FREE YOUR LIFE FROM FEAR

Jenny Hare is a writer, advice columnist and counsellor who has been *Woman's Weekly*'s agony aunt for 14 years. As such, she frequently receives letters from people for whom fear of many different things – illness, failure, death, relationships, divorce, success – causes huge difficulties. *Free Your Life from Fear* aims to provide people with the tools to overcome these fears, which may really affect the quality of their lives.

Overcoming Common Problems Series

Selected titles
A full list of titles is available from Sheldon Press,
36 Causton Street, London SW1P 4ST, and on our website at
www.sheldonpress.co.uk

Assertiveness: Step by Step
Dr Windy Dryden and Daniel Constantinou

Body Language at Work
Mary Hartley

The Cancer Guide for Men
Helen Beare and Neil Priddy

The Candida Diet Book
Karen Brody

The Chronic Fatigue Healing Diet
Christine Craggs-Hinton

Cider Vinegar
Margaret Hills

Comfort for Depression
Janet Horwood

Confidence Works
Gladeana McMahon

Coping Successfully with Hay Fever
Dr Robert Youngson

Coping Successfully with Pain
Neville Shone

Coping Successfully with Panic Attacks
Shirley Trickett

Coping Successfully with Prostate Cancer
Dr Tom Smith

Coping Successfully with Prostate Problems
Rosy Reynolds

Coping Successfully with RSI
Maggie Black and Penny Gray

Coping Successfully with Your Hiatus Hernia
Dr Tom Smith

Coping with Alopecia
Dr Nigel Hunt and Dr Sue McHale

Coping with Anxiety and Depression
Shirley Trickett

Coping with Blushing
Dr Robert Edelmann

Coping with Bronchitis and Emphysema
Dr Tom Smith

Coping with Candida
Shirley Trickett

Coping with Childhood Asthma
Jill Eckersley

Coping with Chronic Fatigue
Trudie Chalder

Coping with Coeliac Disease
Karen Brody

Coping with Cystitis
Caroline Clayton

Coping with Depression and Elation
Dr Patrick McKeon

Coping with Down's Syndrome
Fiona Marshall

Coping with Dyspraxia
Jill Eckersley

Coping with Eczema
Dr Robert Youngson

Coping with Endometriosis
Jo Mears

Coping with Epilepsy
Fiona Marshall and
Dr Pamela Crawford

Coping with Fibroids
Mary-Claire Mason

Coping with Gallstones
Dr Joan Gomez

Coping with Gout
Christine Craggs-Hinton

Coping with a Hernia
Dr David Delvin

Coping with Incontinence
Dr Joan Gomez

Coping with Long-Term Illness
Barbara Baker

Coping with the Menopause
Janet Horwood

Coping with a Mid-life Crisis
Derek Milne

Coping with Polycystic Ovary Syndrome
Christine Craggs-Hinton

Coping with Psoriasis
Professor Ronald Marks

Overcoming Common Problems Series

Coping with SAD
Fiona Marshall and Peter Cheevers

Coping with Snoring and Sleep Apnoea
Jill Eckersley

Coping with Stomach Ulcers
Dr Tom Smith

Coping with Strokes
Dr Tom Smith

Coping with Suicide
Maggie Helen

Coping with Teenagers
Sarah Lawson

Coping with Thyroid Problems
Dr Joan Gomez

Curing Arthritis – The Drug-Free Way
Margaret Hills

Curing Arthritis – More Ways to a Drug-Free Life
Margaret Hills

Curing Arthritis Diet Book
Margaret Hills

Curing Arthritis Exercise Book
Margaret Hills and Janet Horwood

Cystic Fibrosis – A Family Affair
Jane Chumbley

Depression at Work
Vicky Maud

Depressive Illness
Dr Tim Cantopher

Effortless Exercise
Dr Caroline Shreeve

Fertility
Julie Reid

The Fibromyalgia Healing Diet
Christine Craggs-Hinton

Getting a Good Night's Sleep
Fiona Johnston

The Good Stress Guide
Mary Hartley

Heal the Hurt: How to Forgive and Move On
Dr Ann Macaskill

Heart Attacks – Prevent and Survive
Dr Tom Smith

Helping Children Cope with Attention Deficit Disorder
Dr Patricia Gilbert

Helping Children Cope with Bullying
Sarah Lawson

Helping Children Cope with Change and Loss
Rosemary Wells

Helping Children Cope with Divorce
Rosemary Wells

Helping Children Cope with Grief
Rosemary Wells

Helping Children Cope with Stammering
Jackie Turnbull and Trudy Stewart

Helping Children Get the Most from School
Sarah Lawson

How to Accept Yourself
Dr Windy Dryden

How to Be Your Own Best Friend
Dr Paul Hauck

How to Cope with Anaemia
Dr Joan Gomez

How to Cope with Bulimia
Dr Joan Gomez

How to Cope with Stress
Dr Peter Tyrer

How to Enjoy Your Retirement
Vicky Maud

How to Improve Your Confidence
Dr Kenneth Hambly

How to Keep Your Cholesterol in Check
Dr Robert Povey

How to Lose Weight Without Dieting
Mark Barker

How to Make Yourself Miserable
Dr Windy Dryden

How to Pass Your Driving Test
Donald Ridland

How to Stand up for Yourself
Dr Paul Hauck

How to Stick to a Diet
Deborah Steinberg and Dr Windy Dryden

How to Stop Worrying
Dr Frank Tallis

The How to Study Book
Alan Brown

How to Succeed as a Single Parent
Carole Baldock

How to Untangle Your Emotional Knots
Dr Windy Dryden and Jack Gordon

Hysterectomy
Suzie Hayman

Overcoming Common Problems Series

Is HRT Right for You?
Dr Anne MacGregor

Letting Go of Anxiety and Depression
Dr Windy Dryden

Lifting Depression the Balanced Way
Dr Lindsay Corrie

Living with Asthma
Dr Robert Youngson

Living with Autism
Fiona Marshall

Living with Crohn's Disease
Dr Joan Gomez

Living with Diabetes
Dr Joan Gomez

Living with Fibromyalgia
Christine Craggs-Hinton

Living with Grief
Dr Tony Lake

Living with Heart Disease
Victor Marks, Dr Monica Lewis and
Dr Gerald Lewis

Living with High Blood Pressure
Dr Tom Smith

Living with Hughes Syndrome
Triona Holden

Living with Nut Allergies
Karen Evennett

Living with Osteoarthritis
Dr Patricia Gilbert

Living with Osteoporosis
Dr Joan Gomez

Losing a Child
Linda Hurcombe

Make Up or Break Up: Making the Most of Your Marriage
Mary Williams

Making Friends with Your Stepchildren
Rosemary Wells

Motor Neurone Disease – A Family Affair
Dr David Oliver

Overcoming Anger
Dr Windy Dryden

Overcoming Anxiety
Dr Windy Dryden

Overcoming Back Pain
Dr Tom Smith

Overcoming Depression
Dr Windy Dryden and Sarah Opie

Overcoming Guilt
Dr Windy Dryden

Overcoming Impotence
Mary Williams

Overcoming Jealousy
Dr Windy Dryden

Overcoming Procrastination
Dr Windy Dryden

Overcoming Shame
Dr Windy Dryden

Overcoming Your Addictions
Dr Windy Dryden and
Dr Walter Matweychuk

The Parkinson's Disease Handbook
Dr Richard Godwin-Austen

The PMS Diet Book
Karen Evennett

Rheumatoid Arthritis
Mary-Claire Mason and Dr Elaine Smith

The Self-Esteem Journal
Alison Waines

Shift Your Thinking, Change Your Life
Mo Shapiro

Stress and Depression in Children and Teenagers
Vicky Maud

Stress at Work
Mary Hartley

Ten Steps to Positive Living
Dr Windy Dryden

Think Your Way to Happiness
Dr Windy Dryden and Jack Gordon

The Traveller's Good Health Guide
Ted Lankester

Understanding Obsessions and Compulsions
Dr Frank Tallis

Understanding Sex and Relationships
Rosemary Stones

When Someone You Love Has Depression
Barbara Baker

Work–Life Balance
Gordon and Ronni Lamont

Your Man's Health
Fiona Marshall

Overcoming Common Problems

Free Your Life from Fear

Jenny Hare

sheldon PRESS

First published in Great Britain in 2005 by
Sheldon Press
36 Causton Street
London SW1P 4ST

Copyright © Jenny Hare 2005

British Library Cataloguing-in-Publication Data

A catalogue record for this book is available from the British Library

ISBN 0–85969–927–7

1 3 5 7 9 10 8 6 4 2

Typeset by Deltatype Limited, Birkenhead, Merseyside
Printed in Great Britain at Ashford Colour Press

Contents

Acknowledgements   ix

Introduction   xi

Part One

Stop hiding from fear – it's there to help you   1

Part Two

The 12 symbols and how they free your life from fear   9

 1 A compass: take your bearings   11

 2 A map: make a plan, find a route   21

 3 A golden nugget of wisdom: use your wisdom and
    understanding to dissolve fear   30

 4 A key: find and unlock the way out of any problem   38

 5 A white feather: connect with the spiritual realm and
    your guardian angels   45

 6 A ripening seed: use your creativity to dissolve fear   54

 7 A pair of skates: glide through life smoothly and safely   60

 8 A healing elixir: drink in a new attitude to heal your life   66

 9 A pen and ink: write fear out of your day   74

10 A light: light up your life and banish the darkness of fear
    and depression   80

11 A crystal: changing the vibes in tense situations   88

12 A heart: fill your life with love and wash fear away   97

Part Three

Your gifts, your choices   105

Further reading   110

For my sister Penny Stanway

She is always such an inspiration to me and her enthusiasm
for this book urged me on as it took shape. Her confidence
strengthens mine. She is my dear, much-loved friend.

Acknowledgements

I would like to thank: everyone who has been involved with this book at Sheldon Press, especially the editors, Gordon Lamont, Sally Green and Trisha Dale, for their careful work and their kindness and sensitivity in leading me through it; my agent Charlotte Howard, who is always calm and encouraging, and manages to be sensible without squashing my dreams; Christine Thomas and all my friends who have shared their experience of fear and their ways of coping, who are there for me when I'm scared; my horse Queenie, who drew my attention to the fear I tried to hide and the extent of fear in the modern world and set me on a learning curve of discovery; and Linda Kohanov, Lisa Walters, Ingela Sainsbury and Francesca Moignard-Howarth, who have all helped in our journey through fear to courage.

Introduction

I asked all sorts of people from various walks of life this question: 'What kind of book would you like to read which would really help you and make a big difference to your life?' Over and over the same answer came back: 'A book about how to deal with fear.'

I was surprised. They didn't seem fearful. On the contrary most gave every appearance of being confident and successful. 'Fear?' I asked. 'What kind of fear?'

The answers tumbled out. They talked of the fear that clearly for so many was like a grey cloud encircling or permeating their lives. Or of the periods of anxiety they intermittently or regularly experienced. Of their feeling of vulnerability, however successful or strong they appear or actually are. Fear of illness, failure, death, the meaning (or non-meaning) of life. Of aggression, ill health, relationship problems, divorce, sex or lack of it. Of failure or loss of control at work and, over and over again, depression.

'Write a book that works,' one said. 'Not a textbook I'll give up on in the first chapter, or one of those books full of promises and good sense that you forget the minute you put it down. Write something meaningful and – OK – sensible, like your column, but somehow in a way I can remember and use whenever I need to without having to keep rereading.'

A tall order. But I knew what he meant. I too have started reading some worthy books about fear in the past but found them too complicated to finish. And I've devoured a couple of excellent, very readable ones which have helped at the time but quickly been forgotten.

How could I write a book about dealing with fear in a way that would help instantly, but also stick in the mind to be there ready whenever fear struck again? I thought about it for a long time, knowing there was precious little point in writing another too difficult or easily forgotten book.

As an agony aunt, I've written lots about fear. Problems arise when people are scared, of course. And problems scare people, in so many ways. The more I thought about the different ways fear grabs us and how we can free ourselves from it, the more I was fascinated by its complexity and, paradoxically, simplicity. But how to make the possible solutions and strategies stick in our minds?

Love, I thought initially, that is the answer. Love is the opposite of fear and sends it packing – so maybe just remembering to love is the big fear-buster? My last book was about choosing love – how we can manifest it in ourselves and our lives by positive thinking and actions.

I mentioned this to a friend who I knew had read that book.

'All very well, Jenny,' she said. 'It's a lovely book and I'm sure everyone would like to fill their life with love. But how on earth can we when we're scared? Write about fear,' she insisted, 'how we can get free from it. Then it will be easier to live and love confidently.'

She was right. But am I the right person to write this book they so want, I then thought. After all – I get as scared as anyone else.

'Yes – but you don't let it hang about,' said a couple of people who know me. 'You deal with it. Write about that – write about how you deal with fear and manage to live, most of the time, extremely happily whatever is going on in your life. We want some of it!'

So I thought about how I deal with fear: I use symbols of the abilities I've been given which help me cope with life. And I suddenly realized that we all have some of the same gifts, plus extra individual ones. By using the symbols for them as I do, every reader would have the same easy and user-friendly strategy for coping with any fear that crops up.

It's so easy to be overwhelmed by fear. You may be the kind of person who copes well with what you see as trivial problems and is only beset with anxiety about life's 'greater' challenges. Or perhaps you rise to the occasion admirably when faced with a major life crisis but get stressed about 'small' things. We're all different and we all have different fear triggers.

But whatever the fear you experience and its effect on you, you have the innate ability to deal effectively with both its cause and symptoms. The symbols help you do just that. And the help starts immediately you think of the symbols.

Sounds too good to be true? I can only tell you that it really does work. And all you have to do initially is to focus on the symbols and ask which one you need whenever fear touches you, whether it's a gentle enough nudge of warning or a vice-like grip of terror.

Please don't be deterred, if you're a very matter-of-fact sort of person, by references to such things as angels and 'energy'. The symbolism works effectively as a fast-acting and easy-to-remember tool whether or not you believe in such things. It quickly sorts through a thousand possible ways to handle uncomfortable or downright crippling fear, taking you straight to the heart of the circumstances and your ability to deal with them effectively.

It works whether you're a believer in God or the metaphysical generally, or think there's no such thing. If you're the latter, for you the symbols will represent innate and learned abilities to manage fear and difficulties and help you bring them into action. If you're the former, like me you may believe the symbolism also sometimes refers to guidance and help flowing into you. Either way the symbols are inspiring and enabling. They help you get in touch quickly, reassuringly and constructively with your fear-managing and -soothing ability and show you how to see and use it practically.

So here it is. The thoughts, strategies, observations and insights that help me when fear attacks and love is threatened or sunk – along with their easy-to-remember, thoroughly efficient and good-to-use symbols, which will stick in your memory and be instantly retrievable as and when needed.

I can't, even for myself, magically dispel fear for ever. It's part of our design to feel fear as it's essentially there to protect us. Ironically but very usefully, my life has been fraught over the last few months. It's as though the universe meant to make sure I remembered just how intrusive and persistent fear can be when it's trying to protect us. I've had to use the symbols myself while I've been writing about them, so I know, all too well, they really do show how to move fear on, or how to use it, as it's meant to be used, as a warning of danger and pay attention to its cause.

Paying attention to fear is something we will need to do throughout our lives. For fear will keep arriving on the scene and every time it does we need to address it, dealing with or ousting it. It's an ongoing process – part of being a real person.

And it feels good to deal with it instead of trying to suppress it or letting it terrorize our lives. When we face fear, courage comes.

To help you free yourself from fear now and whenever you need to in the future, this is for you.

Part One

Stop hiding from fear –
it's there to help you

Fear. We all know the feeling well – it's part of being human.

Fear can come like a bolt of lightning, striking right to your heart, galvanizing immediate action. Or it can be a gentle whisper: 'Hey, you'd better take a look at this.' This is why we were given the capacity to feel fear – for our protection.

But when we see it as enemy instead of an ally, it all goes wrong. Then fear can be a miserably chronic pain that grips and even disables you – body, soul and mind. It can be a spectre that haunts you even when there is actually no reason for it. It can be a habit which – like any addiction, however painful and destructive – you somehow rely on and don't choose to give up.

Across the centuries some causes of fear stay the same. We may, for instance, fear ill health, death, poverty, abuse and attack. And we fear the lack or loss of love, or of self-esteem or the respect of others.

But there are new fears for our time too. More than ever before humankind lives in an international climate of mistrust and we share a common culture and currency of fear.

In the West the still relatively new equality of women and men continues to play havoc as, more painfully and slowly than we'd anticipated, we learn to live harmoniously and lovingly in the still evolving status quo. Our respective roles, once so fixed, are newly diverse and flexible. Traditional ideas on work, sexual identity and parenthood have been turned upside down, and though it's opened up new realms of freedom for us to explore we're struggling to cope with the fresh mix of challenges and responsibilities.

In our busy, stressful, modern world our built-in flight/fight response is on overload. My mailbag is full of pleas for help with coping with fear and fear-based difficulties. When counselling, I help people work through the fears underlying their depression, relationship difficulties and other problems.

Fear can be a grey cloud dimming your life or intermittent periods of painful anxiety. It may be a feeling of extreme vulnerability. It may transmogrify into anger, rebelliousness or bitter resignation. It may lie behind a mask of depression or addiction, chronic stress or fatigue. We all feel fear. Weak or strong, introvert or extrovert, unsure or confident – fear affects us all.

But fear can free us from perils and negativity

The first step in freeing our lives from these negative conditions is to recognize the benefits of fear and work with them. As hard as you try to run away from fearful feelings, you don't escape them – they move with you like a shadow. They want to help – that's why, like all animals, we have a built-in fear mechanism. It's there to protect us.

The trouble is, we're taught early on that fear is a bad thing and we need to fight or ignore it: 'Be brave.' 'Don't be a baby.' 'There's nothing to worry about.'

So we get very good at being scared of fear itself, and we learn to distrust our own emotions and responses too. We try to squash fear and in so doing ignore or run away from what caused it in the first place.

And the friendly ally, in desperation, shadows our lives until we *do* listen and heed the warning.

There are many ways to run away. You may be the kind of person who throws yourself into work, convincing yourself you need to be there all hours of the day and even focus on it for much of your leisure time. Or you keep busy another way – filling your diary with things to do in an effort to leave no time to address, let alone resolve, what troubles you. You may try to blot out worries by concentrating on television or other entertainment, or drown them with alcohol or other drugs. Some sink into a numbing depression. Some break down. But the faster and further you run or the deeper and darker the place you dig yourself into, the more fear will keep right on clutching at you until you face it and say, 'OK – I'm listening. What's this about?'

The instant relief

The minute we face fear and assess the danger it's warning us about, we feel better. Fear, relieved, retreats. Sometimes it's hardly anything anyway. Literally nothing to worry about and the fear, reassured, will disappear completely. Yes – once you learn and remember to do it – it can be as simple as that. At other times there is more cause for concern, and the fear and the problems it's drawing your attention to may not be dealt with so easily.

We are all vulnerable, even the strongest and bravest, and like everyone else you're certain to find some of the things that happen in life pretty challenging or even daunting.

This is where your gifts come in

The wonderful truth is, we humans have a simply brilliant range of abilities to cope with whatever life throws at us or we get ourselves into. *You* have this range of abilities, in your own unique mix, to enable you to deal with any fearful situation positively, calmly and constructively. As soon as you use the right gifts for the particular fear, it will dissolve or become something you can comfortably manage, regaining personal peace and, hugely importantly, the knack of being able to sleep even in the midst of difficult times or even trauma.

You *can* free yourself from fear – by seeing it as your protector and dealing with dangers as they present themselves. This way we can use our original flight or fight response using all the kinds of intelligence we are blessed with but without actually, except in very rare instances, running away or lashing out.

Use your intelligence and take control

It sounds easy but, as you know, somehow it often isn't. Even as an advice columnist and counsellor, like everyone else I can succumb to fear and I used to sometimes find myself wallowing helplessly before I eventually remembered I knew how to sort it out. And then, however competent I became at coping with my own fear and helping others with theirs, fear would pretty soon jump back with a flourish and there I'd be again – at its mercy, all the well-meaning advice forgotten while once again I got stuck in fear until I went through the remembering process again. It was a long, tortuous way round and I'd often get frustrated and think, there has to be a quicker, easier way to deal with fear – but how?

Eureka!

Then, on a course with a bunch of teachers, the tutor took us through a guided visualization of a journey. On it I had one of those amazing satori moments of enlightenment and it was the first step in a new understanding, which transformed the way I deal with fear and will free your life from its clutches too.

Gifts that symbolize our inborn gifts and abilities

I was already used to meditating but hadn't tried visualization. The others had never tried this kind of thing at all and were sceptical and cynical about the idea. Anyway, we all followed the tutor through the visualization and, towards the end of it, he told us we were now to sense we were being given a gift to help us with our current situation. My gift – in my imagination I could see and feel it in my hand – was a crystal. At the end of the meditation, two of the others revealed they had also received crystals, while the others had received various other gifts. I remember one spoke of an apple and the reassurance she could continue to earn her living; another told of a light and a sudden vision of how he could deal with a current problem in his life. One of the others received insight into her relationship fear with the gift of a small golden heart – a symbol, to her, of her wish and ability to accept her partner's marriage proposal.

The meditation had a profound effect on us all. Whatever our respective gifts, every one of us was astonished at how apt it was for our own particular situation. The gifts helped us see how we could resolve or manage our current problems and realize that we possessed the ability to do this.

Years later, I've come across this visualization many times in various versions. I've taken many people, both counselees and friends, through it myself. It is always powerful and each person's gift has a special meaning for them, always illuminating and often deeply helpful.

Once we know the visualization, we can use it again whenever we need answers, solutions and strategies for dealing with fearful situations. Over the years following my first experience of the journey, I have been given many gifts. They are always apt and they always symbolize an ability to deal with the situation I already have, bringing it to my attention just when it's needed. Twelve of the gifts are abilities we all have and together they form a strong, comprehensive store of strategies to deal with every kind of fear.

Some think we're reminded of the appropriate gift in this way by another dimension – a guardian angel, perhaps, or a higher power. I can't dispute this – perhaps we are. Or perhaps our subconscious, well aware of the ability we need to recognize or remember and use, provides a symbol of it that we can quickly understand and in future call instantly to mind. For the gifts are extraordinarily powerful symbols of an available way of coping with a situation that is bothering us. The gift we are given at any one time refers to information we already have, part of the life-survival kit we were born with and constantly add to over the years. The attention-grabbing symbol immediately draws out this inner wisdom. It can provide an instant solution, or start a chain of thought.

If you are not used to meditating or 'reading' symbols, please don't dismiss their use as frivolous. They are very real psychotherapeutic tools. You don't need to believe in God or any religious faith. The symbolism can work whether you believe in a higher power, other dimensions and the metaphysical or only in proven science and the reality of the world according to the usual five senses.

In the following chapters we'll take one symbol at a time. All 12 symbols, individually and in combination, are catalysts. Your choice will be the exact choice you need for this time. It will:

- point to techniques and strategies for managing your current fear usefully and freeing your life from non-constructive fear;
- remind you of your ability to put them into practice assertively and courageously.

You may wish to suspend disbelief and visualize the gifts as real things or, if you're sceptical, think of them purely as symbols. Whichever, all you have to do is to imagine the symbols and let their personal meaning for you come to mind. However you prefer to categorize them, the symbols are stunning visual metaphors, available and of use to all. Very importantly for me – and everyone I know who uses them – the symbols we visualize are beautiful and at the same time familiar and comfortable to have around. Every time you are given one to use, even when you've used them over and over, be aware of your feelings and be thankful. Sense welcome on both sides, as though the gift is as happy to welcome you into its company as you are to have it here with you. This is expression and appreciation of the love we have for our abilities and talents – our so often unrecognized personal power.

5

As we first sense and then use them, the gifts dance with reassurance and confidence. They seem to emanate energy – and I believe that perhaps they actually do. Certainly they trigger new or renewed belief in ourselves that we can cope well with life, dealing effectively with worries and managing problems effectively.

When the gifts will help you

You can call for a gift or the right combination of gifts whenever:

- You are frightened, whether or not you know the reason for the fear.
- You need to know whether the fear is sensibly protective or an unnecessary fear out of control.
- You are pressured and stressed.
- You are worried or anxious.
- You are suffering from negative emotions, such as anger and confusion, and you don't know why.

The symbol that's right for the problem or situation will come into your mind as soon as you ask for it, and you will begin to understand how to deal with whatever is worrying you, or what it is you need to pay attention to for your safety.

Although I give guidelines for dealing with some specific fears, the symbols will also have other, individual meanings for you. With any fear, let the symbol that comes to mind draw you to what you need to know.

Remember: fear is a useful early warning system. Pay attention to its message and you will learn the art of freedom. Fear is your ally, not an ogre. 'Beware' doesn't necessarily mean something is wrong – it is a call for you to be aware.

Dealing with fear as a matter of course becomes an easy habit when you use the symbols. They are easy and pleasant to use, very practical and can help transform your life.

The 12 main gifts we have are all-powerful and transforming and so I wasn't sure which order to put them in. They are all treasures and each has its own unique mix of ability and power. So, if you feel drawn to one particular chapter, don't feel obliged to start at the beginning of this book and follow the chapter order. Play is an essential component of how you approach the symbols, and so is enjoyment – go ahead and read what appeals to you, and see what happens!

Part Two

The 12 symbols and how they free your life from fear

1

A compass: take your bearings

Feeling lost? Confused? Do you need a new direction? Or are several new directions beckoning, leaving you unsure which one to take? Wherever we are in life, whatever is happening to and around us and no matter how confused or helpless we may feel, we always have the ability to take stock of the situation. The image or gift of a compass is readily available to remind you to say, 'Hold on a moment – let's just get our bearings and think calmly.'

It prompts us to take a fresh look at where we are and see how we can deal with our fears, dissolving or successfully managing their causes so that we free ourselves from them, enabling us to enjoy life, even in difficult circumstances.

Or, if we can and want to take a new direction, the compass is invaluable for reminding us that the best journeys start from a sound base; assessing where we are now grounds us and our fears in the best sense of the word, enabling a sound, confident starting point.

When major life changes are currently impossible, thinking of the compass helps us appreciate the good in the situation and look for opportunities we may not yet have seen to build tolerance, harmony and happiness within it for ourselves and others.

Seeking the truth of your situation, now

The compass is also for when you've lost your sense of purpose or direction. You find yourself standing still or circling fitfully. Peaceful it certainly isn't. You feel lost and your life is probably problematic. You can't see a way out – and that's scary.

It could happen when you're not happy with your work or some aspect of it but don't know what to do about it. Or you're unhappy in your personal life. Terrified of being stuck, uneasy about making changes.

I could have done with a compass a few years back, before I knew about the gifts we have, when my life seemed to be going round in an endless circle of confusion, uncertainty and self-doubt. I'd pour it all out to my friend Chris, and she'd patiently help me explore my thoughts, fears and frustration. Until, that is, she realized we were going over and over the same stuff and not getting anywhere. 'Jenny,' she said. 'I've got this impression of you swimming round and round in a muddy pool. You can only see what's immediately in front of you. There's no way, at this rate, you're going to move on.'

I was lucky to have her insight. She acted like a compass. Immediately I saw the muddy pool and there I was, swimming round and round. The vision jolted me back to positivity. With the help of a counsellor I took a long, understanding look at the circumstances and behaviour that had led me to this point. Fear vanished as my understanding and insight grew. Courage stepped in to help me change what needed to be changed and move on without the past haunting me.

We don't always have a friend available who has the understanding, wisdom and sheer time to assess a situation and face us with the reality. But we do have a built-in ability to take stock for ourselves. When, later, I was given a compass as a symbol of this ability, I realized it meant we don't have to belabour friends and even bore the pants off our own selves endlessly retracing the ramifications when we're stuck or lost. The compass shows us exactly where we are and where we can go.

The compass and leadership

The thought of it can also help us get to grips with a situation and realize we don't necessarily have to wait for someone else's lead to move on. I sometimes use the symbol of a compass to give a sense of personal confidence and leadership. The meaning was brought home to me graphically on a 14-mile walk one late summer afternoon.

We were lost in a dense and increasingly dark pine forest. The track into it had been straight as a die and intersected by others, equally straight, at strict 90-degree angles. We assumed if we kept going we would swiftly cross the wide swathe of the forest's width.

But the track began to curve to the left, almost imperceptibly at first and then in a more obvious sweep. We'd have to take a right – but none appeared for half a mile or so. At last we saw a turning and hastened up it, all too aware the day was shortening fast, but instead of coming to the far edge we found ourselves at a crossroads of six tracks. Not knowing the extent of the first track's curve, we had no idea which one to take.

I waited for my companion Peter to work it out. He'd always been our route planner and leader as he's technically minded and good at mapreading. But minutes passed and it dawned on me that he was not only confused but also panicking slightly as he struggled to sort out the right way forward. I became frightened too – the prospect of staying lost in a dark wood with dusk falling was alarming. Thankfully I stopped myself from urging him to hurry up as I realized the problem. His eyesight depends on his glasses. They were smeary with rain and though he kept trying to dry them they misted up again within seconds. Our lack of a torch didn't help. He simply could not see the map properly. There was nothing for it – I would have to get us out of this myself.

'Have you got the compass?' I asked.

'Yes – here.' He handed it to me and reminded me how to line it up on the map.

It gave me confidence. OK. If this is North and we've walked there, and there, we are here. There was just enough light for me to make it out.

'OK,' I said. 'This is the path we need.'

The compass not only empowered me to lead us through the wood by making sense of our position on the map, but just holding it in my hand and placing it on the map gave me the confidence to use it, read the situation accurately and see the best way forward.

Soon the path led us out of the forest and we made our way more easily in the remaining light of early evening through the country-side to the village where we'd parked the car.

We made it. I hadn't expected or wanted to be leader but the compass enabled and inspired me. And so it often does, metaphorically, in other situations where I feel fazed or muddled.

You and your compass

You hold it in your hand. It fits snugly in the palm, round, comforting. You know it symbolizes your innate ability to take a thorough rain check on your current orientation. From this sound base of knowledge and awareness, you see exactly the various ways you can fare better at this place, or which directions you may consider taking from it. As well as giving you a unique sense of perspective and all-round opportunity, the compass enables you to plot the next phase of your life calmly.

How to use your compass

If you've been going round and round in circles, panicking in a maze of dead-end alleyways or are plain immobilized with fear, *be still* and *stop worrying* while you use the compass. You don't have the time or the emotional capacity to be lost for long and you don't have to be. But to stop procrastinating and move on you need to focus on your position and bearings and this is where the compass is your ally and catalyst.

- Think of a compass and own it as yours. Hold it in your hand. Feel it. See it.
- What does it mean to you? How does it relate to you and your situation?
- How will it help you?

Remember:

  There may be no immediate answers. Realizations and insights into the meaning of the compass for you, and how you can use it to help you see your circumstances clearly, may take time. Think of the compass to remind yourself you have the ability to get to grips with your situation over the next few days or weeks. If you've picked the compass, it has called out to you: 'Use me! I will help you.' Don't resist it. Welcome it, even if at first you can't see how it will help. It will.

Now take your bearings, face the fears that are floating around, address their causes and see them blow away.

Your immediate circumstances

Imagine or better still draw a huge circle to represent the boundaries of your situation. Sense where you are in it and notice all the other key players – family, colleagues, friends – whoever is involved in the aspect of your life that's stuck or blocked. Put them firmly in place – spaced out or clustered together as seems right. If you see yourself running around aimlessly or from one individual or group to another, searching for answers, ink yourself in firmly or, in your mind, stick yourself down with some glue. You are going to keep *still*.

Now draw a bubble in your favourite colour around yourself. Just as the compass has North as its main focus around which everything can be measured, so you are the pivotal point of your circumstances here, now. You cannot perhaps change the way others are fitting into the picture (or not fitting as the case probably is) but you can make changes to your position, your attitude, your practical and emotional actions and responses.

You are the axis of your life and you are at the controls!

Now the fun bit:

- Write down, in the circle, whatever impressions of the situation come into your head. Do it quickly, not stopping to mull them over – just jot them down wherever you like.
- Radiating out from the centre of the circle and all around it, jot down:
  1 Possible ways to fix elements of any stresses or problems and to help yourself find in-depth understanding.
  2 Possible directions you can take either to remove yourself from the circle completely or to find a better direction inside it.

You have made a therapeutic picture to help you see the situation in perspective. The compass attitude enables you to stand back and be objective. Take a long look at the picture. No worry, no frustration, just clear observation.

The current picture
Familiarize yourself with your bearings by living with the picture for a while.

- Look at it often.
- Ask yourself how you feel about it.
- What suggestions for improving it come to mind?

Change the dynamics
When you feel ready, write a list of five things you could do to change the dynamics of the situation to make it a more comfortable place to be for you and others. How can you improve the all-round atmosphere and harmony?

Let ideas come into your mind. Write everything down – even if it seems silly or meaningless. Your subconscious is *not* silly. Remember the world's top creative teams brainstorm ideas all the time. Thousands are irrelevant and don't get taken up but by letting them flow uncritically you let the good ones come through too. They are like gems. You'll spot them and be dazzled. Treasure them as you explore the possibilities they open.

Where now? Where next?

Once you've a clear perspective on your circumstances now and see how to improve them, you may not wish to move on.

You are an amazing human being – totally unique. Maybe your blueprint doesn't include genius or burning ambition but that's OK – join the vast majority of us! It doesn't mean you aren't leading or can't lead a fulfilling, worthwhile life. Often the quiet, uncelebrated lives are the richest in the happiness stakes and, however unsung, the most rewarding. What you may need first is to start relearning to look out for and feel joy in your immediate life. Start noticing all kinds of little things that please you. Pay attention to them and to the feeling they inspire.

What sense is activated?

We're often out of touch with how we feel. So think of the compass again to get in touch with how you're feeling. Register with all your senses – including the sixth, your intuition and seventh, your awareness of your spirituality – imagining you have them even if you don't believe you do.

Really enjoy getting back to base like this. Gradually you'll notice the magic of life more and more. The love hidden in a friendship or just in a passing smile. The beauty of light falling on a wet pavement. The satisfaction of being able to keep ourselves warm and fed with a roof over our heads. Little (maybe huge) realizations like this are the foundation of happiness.

Feel the warmth and love inside yourself in this moment and others will, perhaps unknowingly, be infected by it. Let your good cheer and understanding out and it will light up others' lives – it's like a wave, radiating round your home and out into the world – who knows how far your influence will go? You – and every one of us however quiet and simple our lives – have the ability to change the world. Boring? I don't think so!

Your fear-busting power

Look at your 'Where I am' diagram and you are where you should be, living *now*. No fretting about the past or the hazards of the future – your focus is on the true picture, with yourself at the centre.

Incidentally, I'm not advocating an egocentric 'me' culture. Of course you'll consider the others who feature. But you can only be fair to them if you are true to yourself.

Once you stop and are still, you are in a position to take control of yourself and to some extent that will allow you to influence your circumstances too. Just by changing your attitude to positive, you will beneficially affect what's going on around you, even if at first you can't see how it's working.

No more running away from dragons

As signalled by the compass, your ability to live in and manage the moment is powerful. You are powerful. When you centre yourself on the reality of now, instead of running away from dragons of the past or chasing after mirages in the future, you release your energy to work for your well-being and the general good. It's automatic. And so is the feeling you'll have of a blissful new freedom from fear.

When you are present in your circumstances you see clearly any fears you may have which are fully or partially blocking you from enjoying the present and going forward smoothly. You may need insights into the past to unclog them – this is constructive and not the same as endlessly churning up old ground. With clear vision – perhaps with the help of a counsellor – you can start to see to the heart of things and, once aware of how you were affected, leave it behind so you can go about the business of living unfettered and free to be the real, best you.

The courage of now

Using the compass to connect with where you are now and how you're feeling puts you in a great position to assess how fulfilling the situation is, what if any changes you would like to make and how you see your future.

It can be scary to focus on the present but these qualities will surface to help:

- *Courage*: To be courageous you actually need some fear – you can't show courage if you aren't fearful! And the bravest people who make the most amazing differences to the world are often those who can also fully feel the zap of fear. Knowing it enables them to face it. Confronting it kick-starts bravery. The greatest wimp can also be the greatest hero.
- *Determination*: Situations, relationships and the past that got you here can all be complicated. You need determination to see them clearly, unravel strands and get them in perspective. Your inbuilt compass is there to help. As you get a true sense of the present, you can start to look for the right direction. It may not be apparent at first, but a general direction will appear if you persist and, when it does, follow it intently.

Don't wait for life to get better, make it better now

A lot of the fear in this world comes from unrealized dreams or, worse still, not having any dreams. You want life to be wonderful, but fear it never will be. You're scared others are having a better time, making more money or leading more successful lives and you wallow in procrastination and apathy which make you more and more scared.

Take a look at the compass. Where are you now? Make two lists, one of things you can do; one of things you enjoy – five of each. For example: I can drive, I can type . . . I enjoy chatting with friends, I enjoy relaxing in my pretty living room. Now give yourself some praise and a big hug. You're doing great.

Or did you struggle? That's OK – now you can do something to raise your quality of life, right where you are.

1 Think what else you'd like to be able to do.
2 Research how you can find opportunities and develop skills.
3 Arrange to go to college or join relevant groups or courses.

This is a simple way to improve where you are without having to change things radically. Like armchair travelling, it makes you feel good and gives you the courage to book up and go somewhere. Enjoy!

Time and the hour . . .

When you're stuck in a situation – whether you've got yourself into the predicament or been trapped – thinking of the compass helps you live tolerantly in the moment and stay present, with hope in your heart. We all have the ability to do this. The compass is a great reminder.

Once, when I was a kid and didn't know how I could possibly survive a week's exams, for which I hadn't revised enough, fear began to eat me up. My aunt saw how troubled I was. She didn't try to help me cram or somehow do better in the exams, which wouldn't have worked at that late hour. Instead she realized I needed help in facing the fear and getting through it safely and she summed this up by quoting Shakespeare: 'Time and the hour run through the roughest day.' I took her words as true and relaxed into them. Adages are like that – missives of enablement. They've stood the test of time because they make sense and give courage.

So instead of putting all my energy into wishing with a passion the week was over, or giving way to fear and chickening out of taking the exams, I concentrated on each hour of the day as it happened, either focusing completely on the paper I was sitting, or revising calmly, or recharging my batteries without worrying about what I didn't know.

Sure enough, the week passed and, once I'd settled into it, wasn't nearly as bad as I'd thought it would be. I could have done better if I'd worked harder before, of course, but what work I'd put in paid off once I gave it the chance to by not fretting, and my grades were quite reasonable.

Since then those words have helped me through many a difficult time. Living in the moment is calming and strengthening. Use your compass to remind you to be present in your current circumstances, aware, calm and confident that whatever happens you will come safely through, having done your best.

The power of staying present – and the miracle of the morning glory

A friend of mine read the last section and said, 'Exams are nothing. What about people who have to suffer a terrible loss, or are in truly dreadful situations, like a war, where they can't see an end to the suffering? A silly old adage wouldn't be much good there, would it?'

But it *has* helped me through worse things: two tragic bereavements, a loved one falling for someone else and walking out on me, and a four-year stretch when for various reasons I was unable to quit a job I hated. The compass is a first-class reminder that we have the ability to cope positively in the present.

But it's true I haven't experienced anything worse than the above. My friend's words got me thinking about whether the compass and 'time and the hour' would help in a devastating, inescapable situation. Then I remembered this story of a late friend I hugely admired.

A few years ago I read in the paper about an extraordinary exhibition of drawings and went along to see for myself. Around the walls of the large gallery stretched pieces of the old-fashioned kind of cheap toilet paper. On each piece was a drawing of a scene in the Chinese concentration camp where missionaries Dr and Mrs Kenneth McAll were imprisoned during the Second World War. Conditions were of the most basic, and they had no idea when they would be released or indeed if they would ever get out alive. But Kenneth wanted to make a record of life there. He requested permission and was given the only paper that could be spared, a brush and black ink. That the pictures had to be monochrome didn't matter – in fact it was representational as, Kenneth told me later, the ground, the buildings and the people were mostly tones of grey.

I worked my way round, marvelling at how his simple and beautiful Chinese brush strokes illuminated scenes in the camp. I felt as though I were there. When I came to the last one of hundreds I wept. It was a drawing of the barbed wire fencing. Growing up it was a flowering morning glory. Somehow Kenneth had made or procured a brilliantly coloured ink and it shone out from the grey.

Bravely, hopefully, steadfastly those people lived each day of their internment. Like the morning glory, they were indefatigable.

As well as telling a story of hope and courage, the drawings are a testament to the importance of being present, however traumatic the day, the week, the year. If Kenneth hadn't been, he wouldn't have noticed the beauty of the people and the colour, shining so bright, of the morning glory.

I wanted to meet Kenneth McAll and was delighted when he and his wife invited me round. By then he was an elderly man. He was one of the wisest people I've ever met. I asked him how he kept such a brave heart in the prison camp and he said:

> Love, of course, of my wife and for all of us there. And hope and faith we would one day be free to go home. Faith we would go on to the next life if we didn't survive. And the paintings. The paintings were like a life line. They kept me focused on living each day to the full.

The paintings were his compass.

2

A map: make a plan, find a route

You are a work in progress. You are on a journey through your life, constantly discovering your path. Exciting – but frightening too. Doesn't being an explorer take a lot of courage? It certainly does, but each of us has unlimited courage to follow our personal path through life. For every fear that comes up, I believe the courage will come to you so that, somehow, you can cope and move on.

Even in panic or despair, when you feel the opposite of brave, all you have to do is ask for courage and help and then open your mind to their presence. They will come, for life always does move on and you have all the ability you need for your journey through time.

Choosing your way

The map symbolizes a plan of your life. It documents all the places you live in, visit and explore, and shows all the people who inhabit your personal world – plus all the things you do, the effect you have, the impact you make – you'll see how fascinating and complex it is. It also contains information about places you could travel to and directions you could take.

When I was younger, it never occurred to me that I could have a say in what happened, long term. I bounced from one situation to another, enjoying it and maximizing my chances as best I could. But it's quite scary, living that way. Now, whenever there's potential change in the air – and when isn't there? – I know about the internal map we each have – the ability to look at our lives and see the huge extent of the territory we do and could cover.

The map is your life's story

Pore over it for inspiration and information. Then go for it. The part of the world you inhabit is your territory (refer to page 14 for help). From here you can choose your forward path to the best of your ability. There will be hazards and surprises along the way; you'll make some wrong turns but don't be alarmed or defeated by them – there will be plenty of good choices too and overall, if you move in the right general direction, you'll enjoy the journey on the way to your destination.

And there will be many destinations as you travel through various life phases. Aim to enjoy each one as much as possible, seeing the good, taking an interest, surviving bad weather and dancing when the sun shines.

Different versions for different phases

Use the map whenever you're unsure of the route, when you are confused about what you're doing or where you're going, when you feel lost or misguided. Think of your gift of a map to remind yourself of the territory and where you're heading.

You may need to make several maps covering different aspects of your life, for instance for relationships, career and interests. Three essential questions are:

- Where can I go from here?
- Where do I want to go?
- What is the best way to get there?

Making your life map is fulfilling and chases fear away

On the map of your life you can study the territories all around you – the as-yet-unknown as well as familiar features. It's exciting to do but could be scary if you're in a fearful mood. But with your map (and along the way your other inbuilt gifts) you'll face and cope with fears as you encounter them. You'll get to love travelling through your life, and as well as enabling you to travel courageously and confidently, the mapreading itself will be part of the pleasure.

Like reading a real map, or learning any language, it's easy to learn to mapread through life, if you do it a little bit at a time. First, start at home.

- Look at your compass to check your bearings and see where you are on the map of your life right now.
- Start mapping here. Your present circumstances may be the base camp for future explorations or a starting point from which you move on completely.
- Look at what's happened to you – where you've been – and take a wide view of the country all around you, on both sides as well as directly ahead.

- See how much scope there is? So many unexplored territories, and – who knows? – probably many as-yet-undiscovered ones too.
- Or you may want to play safe and take a well-known route through life – there's nothing wrong with that, most of us do.

Difficult territory

There are times when despite our best efforts to mapread safely through life, we find ourselves in troughs of trouble. When this happens don't despair. You *will* feel better in time (see page 19) and you will get yourself back on to a good path again. No life is perfect and the experience of uncomfortable patches helps us appreciate it to the full when we're going through a lovely part of life. Your gifts will help you cope with difficult people and places meanwhile. But if you're repeatedly falling into the same marsh or getting lost in a maze of dead-end paths, check out why this is happening. See page 27. Then put the signposts you've been missing or reading wrong and all you've learned clearly on your map and watch out for them in future.

Don't set your sights too far ahead

What happens to you and the way you experience it will influence your next path and so the best laid plans need to be flexible. You may fluctuate from them even in the short term.

- Go with the flow: be willing and ready to change as seems apppropriate. Listen for direction.
- Watch for clarity of vision.
- Thinking of the map you have been given, use the ability it symbolizes to steer a good course through your life.
- Use it whenever fear warns you to take care or questions your route.

Mapreading through life

All the way through the various stages of your life's journey, think of your map and what it symbolizes for you at this moment. Keep plotting your course. And remember to use all your gifts too. Whenever you're frightened or unsure, ask yourself which gift you need. Whichever comes to mind, focus on it, imagine holding it in your hand and listen for its meaning.

The map is invaluable for keeping you focused on your direction so you see signposts, read them correctly and keep moving steadily and confidently forwards in the direction you want. Stay in touch with your path constantly like this and fear will be your friend along the way – there to nudge you if you're going off track or missing a short-cut or a pleasanter way, there to warn you against going down a dead end, especially a second time.

Listen, watch, use all your senses

Ongoing fear, especially the irrational kind, is exacerbated by ignorance, so by learning as much as you can of your circumstances and various viewpoints you will gain perspective and see clearly what, if anything, needs to be done. Although conscious of your route, be especially conscious of your whereabouts each day, each hour, each moment.

Find the message in your daily route plan. If all is calm and uneventful, appreciate it and feel the life flow that courses through your body and all around you at this moment. You will find fulfilment and establish peace deep within you.

Your ability to read the map of your life

The map eloquently symbolizes the ability you have to set and steer your life, assessing the territory and choosing the route, helped by the signs. Through every stage of your life there will be as many signposts as you need to keep you on the right track. So often we go charging off at a tangent, headstrong in our blindness or arrogance to clear signs telling of a better way. All you have to do is be aware.

Take time to wait awhile, look at your proposed route, open your awareness to the signposts. The signs and the information are there all around you to help you read your life map, and to plot and follow the right path.

There may be only one way forward or you may see there are several possible routes. You have the ability to study the possibilities and choose and follow the best way forward.

Gain a sense of perspective, lose fear

My dad was a very wise man – not perfect of course, like most of us he had a shadow side – but essentially he was a great thinker and carer. If I was perplexed about which way to go or what to do next he'd say: 'Look at it from other vantage points and listen to other points of view.'

So I grew up learning to assess situations by trying to sense how each person involved was feeling, thinking and reacting. I'd look at their options and wonder what would happen if they changed route too. If I was considering a new course, I'd again think of his advice and consider the different possibilities, look sideways down all the potential turnings, envisage what potential hazards there might be along each route.

Talk to fellow travellers

Don't be afraid to seek help from others who have trodden this way before you or are with you now. In most situations you'll find others have gone through similar things. We can always ask for help in reading the signs and planning the best way forward.

You may be saying: 'But doesn't that just multiply fears if you're always thinking what if so-and-so does this or that, or what if I go down this path or that?'

Well, I guess it does. But the fears aren't unpleasant – they're my allies. And if you do the same and suss out the situation and best route forward by looking at it from as many points as possible all around and within it, you'll discover, as I have, that the more comprehensive your knowledge the less frightened you will be. Understanding gives you the firmest foundation possible to deal with what's going on. It also gives you the best chance of predicting outcomes and being ready to deal with whatever happens. *Perspective feels good – all round.*

Your ability to create your own map

Where your particular circumstances and experience are new and unique, so you can't draw on others' experience, you can still make your own life map. It will remind you of where you have been and where you are going and one day your recording of the way may prove invaluable for others.

What fears will the map help with?
- Getting lost;
- Losing the plot;
- Making the wrong choices;

- Not having the confidence to plan your own course;
- Facing change.

Exploring

Sometimes we're forced to explore, sometimes we choose to. Both can be frightening in prospect and actuality. How much better to explore with a map. So look carefully at your current situation. Pore over it. Scrutinize every detail, and stand back to look at the great scheme of things too. Read the signs and ask yourself:

- What does this mean?
- What territory would that route take me through?
- What will it look and feel like if I visit that place?
- What directions will open to view from there, or there, or there?

Know the territory you inhabit and are set to cross on your life voyage as well as you possibly can. Be so familiar with it that even in the dark you can move confidently forward.

A literal example

Last night I got home too late to walk the dog in daylight. I decided to see how far I would get – if possible the whole way round – without a torch. It was cloudy so there was little light from the sky.

At first, near home, the way was so familiar that I walked confidently even though I could only just make out the path beneath my feet. After a minute or two my eyes adjusted and I could see a little more. Should I return via the fields? I was scared of falling or bumping into spiky hedges or trees.

I was, frankly, frightened. 'Why did you have to set out without a torch?' I asked myself crossly. And then I remembered my gifts and wondered if one would come to mind. I asked for the right one. The map immediately presented itself. 'Right,' I thought. 'This will really test what I preach.'

I thought about the map of the area. I could visualize a map of the fields and gateways that lay between me and home. Keeping the marked field boundaries clearly in my mind, I continued. Rags, who is the colour of dusk, was invisible. She trotted around, better able to see or smell her way than me, but returned often to tell me all was well. She gave me confidence and so did the map. I found the way I wanted even though hedges and gates were invisible, virtually until I touched them. I didn't once have to retrace my steps or change direction. I walked as though I could see – because I held the map, constant and clear, in my head.

The map, a symbol of both my knowledge of the route and my memory of the real map, acted as accurately as my eyes. Without calling to mind the symbol, and what it represented for me in that situation, I would probably have been too scared to continue, if I'd even been brave enough to start. Or, in my fearfulness, I could have blundered off the chosen path or fallen or got lost. The symbol of the map connected me with my ability to find my way safely in the dark.

It's so vast, the scope we each have. Exciting but, without a map, it can be as frightening as walking in the country on a starless night. And without a map it's so easy to keep getting lost in a maze, going down the same no-through-roads over and over again. Remembering to use the ability to find your way which the map symbolizes, you won't retrace your steps unless you expressly want or need to for some reason. And instead of hanging about in the same place, wishing you could be somewhere different, doing something different too maybe, you'll have the confidence to map out the areas you want to explore, places you want to go, careers you want to follow, people you want to mix with.

Maps are for inspiration as well as direction. If it's fascinating to pore over a geographical map, just think how wonderful poring over the map of your life will be.

When you wonder if you're off track and have ventured into enemy territory

You know that feeling? One thing after another goes wrong and it feels almost as though you're being targeted. Hostility and arrows fly through the air. What on earth is going to happen next?

It's scary because as well as fearing yet more hazards and mishaps you know full well that negative thinking makes mistakes more likely and has a generally adverse effect on those around us too. So altogether fearful thinking makes negative results three times as likely to be a self-fulfilling prophecy. Perhaps the most effective thought is that we actually change the magnetic field around us and project energy to others.

There's nothing else for it – you've really got to zap this kind of 'I'm having a bad run' fear before it gets the chance to gain momentum.

In specific hostile situations, you might want to consider using a crystal first – something which for me works particularly well (see Chapter 11). But when your whole life's path seems fraught, think of the map and remember your ability to take the whole territory of your life in hand. Take a long, calm look at your current position and what's going on around you. Then carefully consider the various paths you can take from this point on.

- Where are you on the map?
- Are you under attack from people you know or strangers you're meeting?
- Are you doing so much that you're setting yourself up for mistakes or accidents?
- If your health is poor, why is your immune system down? Is there anything about your lifestyle you can change to improve your health?
- Is there a better, safer way forward?
- Can you avoid or make peace with hostile people?

Look for signs and clues. Be ruthlessly honest with yourself. Is it truly not your fault? If you are totally blameless, what can you do to win others, or the situation, round? Or, in your heart, do you realize if you'd acted differently you could have defused things with a little common sense, attention, love and warmth?

You'll probably come up with a clear picture of how you and/or your choice of path directly influence your well-being. It follows that you can make changes to improve your situation, moods and general health. You can deliberately take a positive route forward, if necessary changing course to give yourself and everyone around you the best possible chance of getting on well together and being individually successful and happy too.

The map is particularly useful when you have fears about

- *Your career path or lack of one* Imagine holding a map that is going to help you find direction. Think of the information such a map would contain; for example, possible progressions you could make personally, training courses you could enrol for, a mentor who would help you succeed. Or a sideways or totally new direction: a move to an associated or completely different field, new studies, even a change of geographical area to enable you to find interesting work more easily.

- *An unfulfilling or stuck-in-an-uncomfortable-rut lifestyle* Make an imaginary life map. Cover a huge sheet of paper with things you would like to do, places you'd love to visit, people you'd like to meet. Then think of routes that might take you to some or all of these destinations.
- *Travelling for real* Despite the number of people who travel in their work or on holiday, many are scared stiff of travelling or of getting lost or not being able to find their way to places. Think of the map as a metaphor of your ability to move around the world, finding your way in foreign places and at home, and – should you get lost – your ability to cope and mapread your way back to safety.

Know that with the help of your gifts you have the ability to re-chart your path, changing your behaviour if your presence has been upsetting others, or taking different avenues to be with friendlier people. Read the map. See what the signs mean. Face fears constructively. We are all travellers in time: make your travels through this life as invigorating and pleasing as possible and aim to improve the lot of each person you meet along the road in some way.

You are never lost. Fear not. You can find your way at all times and, often, it is beautiful.

3

A golden nugget of wisdom: use your wisdom and understanding to dissolve fear

You are wiser than you have ever realized. And wisdom, like love, is the antithesis of fear. So if you let your natural wisdom flow it will flush fear away.

The golden nugget of wisdom is a powerful symbol of the ability you were born with to think and act using the knowledge, experience, understanding, common sense and insight you collect and the enlightenment that comes to you as you live. Using this ability empowers you to look into fears and manage or wipe them out.

How to use the golden nugget of wisdom

1 In any fearful or potentially fearful situation you don't understand, imagine you have in your pocket your gift of a golden nugget of wisdom.
2 Delve down for it and hold it in your hand.
3 Feel its weight and worth. Feel how solid and dependable it is.
4 Ask for compassion, insight, empathy, clarification as you need.
5 Know that the answer you need will come from the centre of you, or from a higher power.
6 Listen out for help – be aware. An insight may come into your mind straightaway, but don't expect this for it may come to you later and in an indirect way.

Your own deep wells of knowledge
Every day of your life you are taking in an extraordinary amount of information from all your senses. Your brain stores away most of this in the deepest recesses of your memory where it usually stays. Although with training and practice you could absorb and use more knowledge on a conscious level, the chances are that you don't stretch yourself to do this much.

But the vast stores of detailed knowledge you've automatically accumulated still lie within you, available for you to use whenever you need to call them out.

In addition to this stored knowledge we have a real, practical ability to sense when we are learning something new and helpful, and to pay close attention to it. It can be a valuable tool in developing our thoughts and ideas – a very practical aid alongside our own memories, studies and research.

- The symbol of the golden nugget is a clear reminder to ask for the understanding we need. Asking for wisdom is often a catalyst enabling us to receive it.
- Remember the wisdom you are seeking may not come directly to you but often arrives later, in some perhaps unexpected way.
- It will come – but it's easy to miss it. So when you ask for wisdom and understanding, try to stay aware, or at least tune in and listen often, so that when it arrives you are able to 'read' it.
- Be willing to be helped, too – your attitude makes a huge difference to your ability to accept wisdom.
- Don't just hope for enlightenment; expect it and deliberately attract it by giving rein to your creativity and meditating regularly (see Chapter 6).
- And when knowledge, information or inspiration arrives – welcome it with a generous heart and give thanks.

Wisdom to help manage everyday fears

Fear is a very necessary part of life – a safeguard. But it doesn't have to bind us up and if you watch out for it and follow the steps of fear-busting as a matter of course your life can be free of its painful clutching.

But freedom from fear doesn't mean we will lead fearless lives – it means we will live freely alongside our fears, appreciating their possible worth, evaluating each one carefully and deciding if it's authentic and has a cause which needs paying attention to, or inauthentic and a mirage, in which case it can be dismissed.

Freedom is being in control of fear, not letting it control you

This is fundamental wisdom for personal freedom whatever our circumstances, and yet something we often forget. Last night, for instance, I awoke two hours before the alarm setting, fretting about some minor problems in my life. It took me half an hour to remember what to do. 'Which gift do I need?' I asked. Almost simultaneously came the answer: the golden nugget of wisdom. I imagined it, heavy and solid in my hand. I asked what I needed to know and immediately realized the simple answer: 'The worries can be effectively dealt with in the morning and don't merit or need you to focus attention on them right now.' I also realized that if I slept well now it would help me deal with life tomorrow. I said thank you for the gift and the good sense. Then, imagining the nugget still round and solid in my hand, I drifted off into a wonderfully sound sleep until it was time to get up.

Saying thank you is important.

When we show our appreciation of a symbol and the ability it represents, it boosts our appreciation and feels good in itself. The more we practise using the gifts and the more we give thanks, the easier it is to use them. I thank God because I believe in a higher power, but you can still give thanks if you're agnostic or atheist, or you may like to thank the greater goodness, the universe or simply your own mind. Appreciating our ability enables it.

At times when I'm sure a solution or creative inspiration is almost within grasp but I can't quite get it, I'll ask about it before I go to sleep. If you're not in the habit of doing this, do try it. Simply ask for help with whatever it is you're puzzling over. Then let go of the thought completely and go peacefully to sleep. Often the answer will come as you wake up or will 'ping' into your mind unannounced at some point during the day. Again, you may believe it comes from God or the universal consciousness, or see it purely as a mechanism of your brain facilitated by the question followed by relaxation. Whichever is right – it's extremely useful.

It's so easy to forget we have the ability to deal with fears, however small or large they may be, as and when they arise. The gifts – this time the nugget symbolizing common, already known, sense – remind us to use our ability to listen to our fear and apply the appropriate remedy whenever we're anxious about anything.

How do we know if our feelings, perceptions and even our thoughts are genuine?

I find there are two main ways:

- by taking time to be honest with ourselves, every day;
- by questioning every disturbing feeling we have which has no obvious cause.

Touching base with ourselves – it need take only a few minutes – keeps us in touch with our emotional congruity. Ask: 'Is this feeling reasonable and coming from the immediate situation and influential circumstances?' If so, you have a firm starting point to seek the right way to deal with the fear and other feelings you are experiencing.

Or ask: 'Is this mood harking back to an unconnected experience in the past which has nothing to do with it but is causing me to react incongruously?' If so you're likely to stick a false label on your fear, your other feelings and resultant behaviour, and set off on trails that will lead to confusion and unhappiness. This you'll then blame on the situation you misinterpreted, causing more resentment, or see it as inexplicable, causing more hurt, confusion and a hard-done-by attitude – more, more and more fear.

How essential it is to touch base with the truth of our feelings and circumstances as they pan out through every day.

How can we find and use wisdom to deal with others' foibles and problems?

We're so fearful of others' pain that we try to rescue them – and, you know, we can't. They have, ultimately, to do it themselves; it's the only way. You know that feeling when a friend's in trouble and you so want to say something helpful? Don't – at least not straightaway.

Take time to think of the golden nugget of wisdom and ask for help in knowing what to say or not to say.

Often the very best thing we can do is to listen, warmly and if possible empathetically (you understand how they feel and are feeling with them), or warmly and sympathetically (you feel for them and wish them well).

But surely you can say something?

It depends. Unless you can say something genuinely insightful or helpful, it's much more sensible and helpful to say nothing. Show you're interested, encourage them to keep talking if they wish to, hand them a box of tissues if they're emotional, but don't feel you have to dive in with advice or your experience, or hug them, or wave a magic wand to take their pain away.

You can't take their pain away. But by being there for them as someone they can pass the pain to in some small measure even just for a few minutes, you can help them. If they ask what you think, or wonder if you've had a similar experience so you can compare notes, then it's fine to make it a conversation – but remember, only if that seems very definitely to be what they want. Don't push your story onto them.

You may laugh at me at this point – after all this book is full of advice, isn't it? Yes, but I'm not sitting in your room talking at you. You can pick the book up and read a bit of it at random, work your way through it in your own time or search for an apt chapter as you wish. Or you can think, 'No, it isn't for me', and pass on it. As an agony aunt, I'm constantly asked to give advice – again, it's up to each individual whether she wants to read it, or not. But in person, whether counselling professionally or talking with a friend in difficulty, it isn't usually advice people need but someone to listen and allow them to take stock of the situation, however long it takes, and to enable them to open their own doors of understanding and move through.

Sometimes I'll comment, if I genuinely believe it may be useful or if they ask me to. Often, though, when I ask for the wisdom to help someone who is unhappy, fearful and fraught, the thought comes immediately into my mind: 'Jenny, there's nothing you can say or do here. Just be with them and in so doing you'll carry their difficulty for them as they talk to you.'

People who are trained to be Samaritans learn how helpful listening is; no advice, no personal experiences – they just listen as the caller talks as much or as little as they want. And if the caller doesn't talk at all that's OK – the Samaritan doesn't jump in to fill the gap, but keeps quiet and waits.

> Silence can be warm and welcoming. Silence can be the gentlest of hugs.

Snippets of wisdom wing their way to where they're wanted, when they're wanted

When you do give advice, or say what you think about a situation, think of the golden nugget of wisdom first and wait before you speak. You don't have to speak quickly, jumping into the silence. Something I've learned when I'm counselling is that people like to see you're thinking – it makes them feel valued and safe. It's also a time of 'holding' the problem. For the moment you have taken the burden from their shoulders, lifting their fear away for a while. It won't hurt you and it gives them a time to be calm.

You don't have to say much. Sometimes a few words are all it takes – a few words which have a lot of meaning, insight or comfort; which they will remember easily, so they can think of them at any stage in the future. A few words may land unnoticed in someone's mind and rest there for days, weeks, years and then surface, shining bright.

Keep learning, all your life long

It's easy to be scared that we're not very brainy. But we are, all of us, and definitely, you too. So don't waste time massaging the vanity of such fears with self-deprecating remarks. Instead use the golden nugget of wisdom every day to remind you that you have an amazing brain – a zillion times brighter than the newest, most sophisticated computer technology can even dream of. But nobody can force you to use it. No one can make you learn. You just need to want to, that's all, and you will.

Remember those cathartic times when understanding flowed into you and turning out good work was a real pleasure? Realize you still have the same brain and capacity to use it every bit as charismatically, every day of your life now and, health willing, for the rest of your life.

You can help your learning and breakthrough periods of absorption and comprehension along in many ways. For instance:

Benefit from others' thinking and philosophy

We fear we are wasting precious life being couch potatoes or performing mindless activities; but we keep doing it anyway and the fear festers and leaves us discontented or, at least, with a feeling of being unfulfilled and missing out. Free yourself completely from this fear in a few fell swoops.

Read selectively

By all means enjoy the occasional blockbuster for sheer enjoyment and relaxation but, in general, programme your reading very carefully. Read to know, to learn, to digest information and for inspiration too. A student of C. S. Lewis told him: 'My father said: "We read to know we are not alone."' Do the same. Read to connect with the world – it's *your* world, your brotherhood and sisterhood, your chance to pick up and use the wisdom of those who have trodden this path before you.

Other media

Never watch something on television you realize straightaway is empty of understanding or fun for you. Don't listen to piped music that does nothing for you. Remember that everything you take in will stay in – so don't clog up your brain with cotton wool. Let everything you choose to watch and listen to be beneficial, informative, mind-enhancing or at least, if you want to completely chill out, pleasantly soothing.

Learn something new every day

So my father told my sister and me. Hold the golden nugget of wisdom often. Remember to connect your brain so you can connect with your understanding and compassion. And add to your inner wisdom every day by taking in and learning something new. Notice it and memorize it. If you come across nothing new, go and find something, every day. Keep your brain cells working and they'll thrive and keep renewing their full complement.

Think constructively, deeply, sideways

It's so easy to take things at face value, and this explains the kind of fear we experience when we think we know something but feel it doesn't make sense. Banish this kind of fear in any or all of these ways:

- Develop an enquiring mind.
- Mull things over. Ask others' opinions. Talk, debate, inspire and be inspired. Good conversation is thought-provoking and often illuminating. Ride it like a truly good horseman rides his horses – sensitively, fairly, with understanding, aiming to get the best from the minds of each person and yourself.
- Brainstorm ideas. Don't fear that people will laugh at your off-the-wall ones. They may, but that can be fun. Some of the best ideas come when you set your mind free to play, wander sideways and be zany.
- Waste no time and energy if you wake worrying in the middle of the night. Use your wakefulness to think – logically, practically, obliquely and deeply. Be glad you have a little quiet time to think. Hold the nugget of wisdom to make the moments shine golden too. And then purposefully drop into sleep and let your subconscious take over.
- Be aware there are many kinds of intelligence. Intellectual, scientific, mathematical, creative, practical, technical, streetwise, emotional, intuitive, spiritual, environmental, linguistic, connecting with other people and animals … the list goes on and on. Don't demean yourself and squash your natural intelligence by saying you're hopeless at this or that – maximize and give thanks for your talents by becoming more aware of them and encouraging them to expand.
- Every day, use your golden nugget of wisdom to remind you to seize the day. You and it are only here once. Seize the opportunity and the joy and you will be free from negative fear.

4

A key: find and unlock the way out of any problem

It's frightening to feel blocked or trapped, or to be convinced there's a solution to a problem but fail to find it. The key is a symbol of your intrinsic freedom, and of freedom from fear.

You have the power to open doors in your thinking and vision that will open doors for you in real life and solve puzzles in practical ways. You can find the right key. Such potential!

When we're children we see adulthood as a world of freedom and think it's going to be a doddle. But when you grow up you soon realize that things don't always work out and life can be difficult. You can then choose to be daunted by problems, closed doors and confusing situations. Or you can choose courage, optimism and a bright outlook, working out how to cope with challenges and also encouraging, cherishing and relishing all the wonderful aspects of life.

There is always a key to a puzzle, to open doors to other places, unlock safes of information, find a solution or free you from oppression.

Imagine holding the key in your hand

Sense its reminder that you hold the keys to your life – a comprehensive range of abilities to unlock barriers and find solutions. Whenever you're frightened because you feel blocked or confused, remember you can find the right key.

Whenever you're constricted by circumstances or your attitude, the key is there to remind you that you have the power to free yourself. Even when circumstances can't be changed – because of responsibilities, for instance – you can always free your soul. It is your God-given right and an inbuilt ability. Know that you are not a hostage to fortune but a free spirit. And very often you can open doors to set you free from the constrictions of life too.

How the key can banish fears and open doors to freedom

The key and your career

Most of us have to work and not everyone is lucky enough to find a job they love. So we're likely to spend part or all of our lives working at something we'd essentially rather not be doing – and that can seem like a trap. As an agony aunt I've seen this to be a frequent cause of depression. Those who dislike or, at worst, hate their work harbour the deep-seated fear that they are wasting precious years of their life. They fear there is no way out, or, if shown various ways out, they fear leaving the prison and/or going into new territory.

But we are fortunate, these days, that working lives can be flexible. Look for a key and how you can open doors and you'll usually find a way into work you do enjoy.

There are more options too. Working from home is a very real possibility for many people. Flexitime can transform working life. Job sharing, part-time work, sabbaticals, training courses – research the option that would suit you – go for it if it's right. You are free to look, and if you really want to do something you feel is the way forward and within your capability, there will be a way.

Emotional fears

Relationships vie with work as one of the greatest areas of fearfulness. If we feel stuck in a relationship or marriage, it frightens us, and if this fear is allowed to grow it can become so claustrophobic the only way to escape it can seem to be to quit. Around one in two marriages ends in divorce and a far greater proportion of live-together relationships break up. Fear is always involved and fear, being the opposite of love, eats love away. Couples have so many possible fears. You can fear you're not in love any more, your sex life isn't so good, your partner doesn't love you or you don't love them, you're always rowing, you're not compatible – all kinds of fears.

But there is one huge master key to all these difficulties. It's remembering that the love you share is a living thing, fluctuating and adjusting throughout your life together. No relationship is perfect and all couples sometimes have differences and difficulties much like yours. Accept this – expect it – and you can take each fear as it comes and act on its cause constructively or dissolve it rationally, whichever is appropriate.

The key at the beginning of any fear, any problem is to face it, think what's best to do and do it

It sounds so easy, but it's not. When we're in a situation like this it's so close we often can't see the way to resolve it. People tell you to talk but you don't know how, or you do and it makes things worse. What then?

Think of the key again and listen to what it's telling you. You still have the ability to heal whatever's wrong, but you need some help and/or some extra sympathy for each other's feelings and the way you're interacting. You can get this help. A phone call will make you an appointment with an experienced relationship counsellor who can help you learn to work through the issues. Or you can read books by couple counsellors. Don't give up on the first book you pick up if you don't like its style; go on to another until you find one that strikes a chord. It's very subjective. I read all the time, but out of 100 books I open only a few are helpful to me. See 'Further reading' for my suggestions but go on your own book search too. You can order any UK-published book at your local library – a wealth of potential understanding and inspiration readily available. The key is your ability to access wisdom, absorb it and develop your own.

Talk to couples who've been together for years and are still devoted and you'll find they have all developed their own relationship wisdom. You can too. You are worth it, so is the partner you love, so is your relationship.

Sometimes it may be too late to save a relationship, or perhaps one or both partners simply feel it's time to move on. It's easy to stay together for years, living in fear of hurting each other or being independent. But the relationship becomes like a prison. In this situation, the key may symbolize your ability to face the fact that it's no longer right to be together, talk about it kindly and sensitively and, together, work out the best way to part and go your separate ways. A key to coping with the pain of separation is to remind yourself repeatedly that, impossible as it now seems, you will heal and life will be good again.

The key to personal development and fulfilment

You might feel trapped because you don't know how to free the creative spirit you know you possess. You long to dance in time to the drummer you hear, but feel as though something is tying you down, holding you back from the freedom to do just that.

When we're scared of our creativity we create our own ties, pretending someone else or some circumstance is dictating our lack of time or energy to follow our muse. That way we hide from the responsibility of it being up to us.

Face the fear. Use the key to help you see what's blocking you, locking your spirit in. Use the key – your innate ability – to oil the lock and open the door so you can free up your talent and start developing it and letting it fly.

My story

I knew I wanted to be an artist – to write and paint. At school I wasn't encouraged and soon doubted my ability. On two occasions in art and English classes the respective teachers laughed at my work in front of the class. They probably meant no harm and I'm sure they had no conception of the harm they did. But they scared me away from becoming my true self and I spent the next 20 years or so doing instead what I thought others expected and I was sure I could deliver. Looking back it was good experience because it led me down all kinds of paths. But through all this, thankfully, I was never quite so scared that I completely lost touch with my creative spirit. I'd write an article now and then (several were published), I wrote television plays (not to see the light of day but good practice!), but it didn't occur to me I could draw or paint.

Then I had the good fortune to work for a man who encouraged me to write. He was in PR and soon sussed out my English was good and that I thought originally, and he promptly started delegating his work to me. At first I was scared: 'Me? Oh no, I couldn't do that.' But his confidence made me look at the fear and realize it was a phantom. OK – so people laugh at our work sometimes – it doesn't mean it's bad, or even if it is, that everything we do is, or that we can't in any case improve and flourish with practice. And so I got going. Pretty soon I had my own PR business, and then one day I finally faced the still persistent fear that I didn't have what it took to be a journalist and write books. I suddenly realized that every press release and trade article I wrote got published so my fear was a phantom. I could do it! I'd simply shut the door on my ability but now I'd faced the fear I was using my inbuilt key to access the blocked areas. I began painting too. It was a shining time!

After a while I found myself locked in another place. Then I had a vision where I clearly saw myself unlocking a door. This was the first time I sensed and used the key as a symbol and recognized its power to help.

By then I was a journalist with several years' experience on a busy regional paper, and currently editing my own section. I'd simultaneously trained as a counsellor and put in several hours a week seeing clients. But I felt burned out and a nagging fear plagued me: fear of boredom at the paper, of wasting time and creative drive. Yet I was even more afraid of how I would get on if I took the plunge and started writing what I really wanted to write – self-help books and fiction too. So I stayed put for a year, becoming more and more unhappy in the office, which wasn't like me at all.

The key and the open door

One day, while meditating, I suddenly saw myself clearly. I was in a large, empty room, trying to get out. I found the key to the lock in the door. I turned it and the door opened. But instead of going through it to freedom I turned away and cowered in the corner, wanting to go through and knowing it was right for me to do so, but far too scared to take that step.

Looking down on myself, I suddenly understood what was going on and why. I felt compassion for my frightened self. Facing the fear caused it to start falling away and my courage started to rise in its place. It took a few weeks more, and then I handed in my notice and went freelance. I needed the freedom of my imagination and opinion unencumbered to be able to fly free – and that image of the key unlocking and opening the door enabled me.

Nowadays, like most creative people, I still get scared often that people won't like what I do. But that's no big deal. Writing and painting are very subjective and there are always going to be some people – lots even – who don't like your work. The key, for me, is mostly to do with keeping my spirit free flowing – unblocked and unlocked. I believe it's the key for most of us. We are all creative in our own way.

Using your key

- Put the key in the lock and turn it.
- Some locks are tricky – you may need to adjust, cajole, coax it.
- Sometimes you need an extra oomph of pressure to find the solution.
- Or you may need to go very gently and sensitively, easing your way to unlocking it.
- When something is locked, if it's right that you should open it you will find the way.
- Keep the image of the key in mind. Eventually you will find how to turn it and open up your understanding.

When research is the key

Scientists use their key ability all the time. They constantly research and think, always seeking knowledge and insights. The key is the sign of an enquiring mind, open to discovery.

Think of the key to let your mind fly, free of fear.

Sometimes something happens that causes a revolution in the way the human world works. The Internet is an example. Original thought was the key to this astonishing new dimension of information and communication. And now the World Wide Web is itself the key for the millions who use it to access the world's fact and fiction.

You may not have such a world-transforming thought, but you do have the key to using your own unique mind. So use it. Exercise your many kinds of intelligence – and don't underestimate yourself.

The key to your self-esteem

Use the key like this and your self-esteem will flourish. Then you will be able to get any situation in perspective, and fear will not be a foe who seems to terrorize or drag you down but the ally it truly is, there to look out for you and help you and willing to disappear when you pay attention to its message and act as necessary.

A key can be the way in or out, the facilitator of motion and the reader of emotion. It can be prosaic and practical or mystical and magical.

You can always ask yourself, in the midst of confusion or conflict, 'OK, I'm stuck – what is the key to this?' Thinking of the key *is* a key. It will allow your brain, heart and soul to seek insight and/or a solution at the deepest, most complex or most piercingly simple level as necessary. It will gear you to thinking logically and sideways, exploring how you can safely open the door to ways forward, look through at them and, as you wish and feel is right, stay put or move forward bravely.

5

A white feather: connect with the spiritual realm and your guardian angels

Whether or not you believe in them, I'd like you to suspend disbelief if necessary and just imagine another dimension with angels who look after us and a higher power who is always there for us. Now imagine you have the inborn ability to connect with their goodwill towards you. You can summon this feeling of safety and protection at any time you need help. Doesn't that feel good?

In fact the ability to create within yourself a feeling of well-being and protection, symbolized by the white feather, is an inbuilt gift we all have.

I believe there is indeed another dimension – perhaps many – and I sense an energy of love. But I remember my dad, an agnostic with as great an interest in science as spirituality, saying, 'Well, of course there could be other worlds and other layers of understanding and being. And even within this vast universe there may be other life and energies that we are unable to make contact with through present scientific means.' But he'd add: 'Equally, there may not be.' However, he was a firm believer in the power of positive thinking to change moods, relationships and situations for the better.

A good friend of mine is a staunch atheist. However, he too likes the idea of having a guardian angel and, though convinced his is a fantasy, tells with enthusiasm that when he imagines it is looking after him his fear becomes manageable and he gets through the difficulty causing it more easily.

So, even if you think the idea of angels is wishful thinking, it doesn't matter; the *idea* itself is a metaphor leading to a more positive frame of mind, which helps you deal with problems and dissolve fear. Quite simply, it works. The white feather is a symbol to lift your consciousness, your practicality and your mood, and can indeed help save you from potentially damaging negativity.

And who knows, even if you believe that what we sense with our physical senses is all there is, in practising imagining the white feather and the intense beauty, joy and love it represents, you may find you start to wonder about other senses. Don't worry if you do – enjoy the wonder of the possibility.

If you are sceptical about angels or spirituality, please remember that every time I mention them or the white feather that symbolizes them, it's a metaphor for your innate capacity to feel secure and protected, however troubled your circumstances.

Why the white feather as a symbol?

Where did the white feather symbol come from? Was it the film, *Forrest Gump*, with Tom Hanks? That certainly put it firmly in the public domain but the notion was around long before. It's very apt as there can be few things purer, brighter, lighter and yet so incredibly strong and with such insulating properties. But I don't see angels as flying human beings with feathered wings – as sceptical friends will tease me. Nevertheless, in times of darkness when I've remembered to think of the white feather, I've had a vision of powerful but gentle wings being folded over me for protection, or underneath me to support me. Even if the problem wasn't quickly resolvable, I felt essentially safe and knew that, somehow, I would cope.

Rita, a deeply spiritual friend, often feels – she insists she actually *feels* – the touch of wings brushing ever so lightly against her when she talks with her angels. And of course many mystics over the centuries have had visions of angels and painted how they saw or understood them to look – and they're usually winged. So who knows? Even if there were no such thing as a spiritual dimension, angels are a great metaphor for protection and peacefulness.

The symbol of the white feather is a good reminder of the strength and capacity for self-protection we have within us, whatever our circumstances. Just think of it and you can call on it whenever you need.

How many times have your angels, real or metaphoric, saved you from danger without you knowing they helped?

Often – probably more than we ever realize – our angels help us unasked. I've had two close-to-accidental-death experiences when it seemed as though an unseen strength stepped in to save me. One happened when my car was out of control on sheet ice and heading for the central reservation at speed. The wheel was locked and the brakes of no effect, and suddenly it was as though someone or something took hold of the car from above and brought it to a stop. As I sat shaking with shock I was aware I'd been helped – snatched back from what was sure to have been a serious and possibly fatal crash.

The other time, I lost my balance on the edge of a sheer drop of 12 feet or more to the tarmac road below. I was falling – there was no way I could wrench myself back and nothing to grab hold of. Again there was the sensation of the momentum being stilled. Somehow I managed to defy gravity and force myself upwards and over to uprightness on firm ground again, but I can only say it felt as though I was lifted. The driving incident I can't explain rationally; I had no knowledge of driving on ice at the time but realize there's a possibility something I physically did in that split second of panic helped save the car from crashing. The fact is that in both cases my silent, nanosecond cry for help preceded salvation.

How many times unbeknown to us do angels, or an inner ability to save ourselves, move us from the path of danger? But angels aren't all about life saving miracles like this – they are round us to help out in all kinds of little ways, day and night. If we ask them to help, there they are. Let's look at night-time first.

Night frights and insomnia

You know the feeling? When you wake up, your heart gripped with fear and maybe you're in a cold sweat too. Perhaps your mind focuses on one worry, or others may follow in swift succession, all demanding attention.

That's exactly what they *are* doing. These issues need attention, that's all. Sometimes this kind of fear can be a boon. Something you need to do that should have occurred to you in waking hours didn't, and your subconscious only manages to bring it to your attention as you sleep, startling you into wakefulness. Occasional night fears like this are beneficial, allowing you to put your whole mind to the matter and decide what needs to be done.

Make the decision or plan, say thank you to your mind for bringing it to your attention and then say to yourself: 'Right, that's dealt with. There's nothing more I can do now – I'm going back to sleep.' But before you do, think of your white feather and ask your angels to take care of the plan and to watch over you as you sleep.

Sometimes if I'm puzzling over something or feel I'm missing something or need guidance, I'll say to them: 'As I sleep or in the days coming up, please will you give me new insights, understanding and direction.'

Why do we tend to sense them more at night? I think it's because our spirituality is freed as we sleep and also when we are newly awake. So we are free then to tune in to their presence and messages.

And in daytime

I believe angels are with us all the time, even when we're too busy or preoccupied to think of them. But it's quite extraordinary how the briefest passing thought and request is followed by something happening that is helpful. Assistance isn't always obvious – it could be as simple as fresh inspiration or hope or trust that encourages or allows all to be well. We can even ask for help with the most mundane things too – doors that seemed firmly shut suddenly open, tricky tasks are tackled more easily, awkward people unfreeze.

Sometimes I've wondered if it's being disrespectful of angels to involve them in such trivial matters but they seem to delight in it. I guess it's much like prayer to the Greater Goodness: God (or, if you prefer, your own mind) likes us to connect and converse and even, when we know it's right that it should happen, to demand. I think the angels are longing for us to recognize them more, too, and plug into their power. I wonder if angels have a sense of humour and think it's fun to help us with small matters.

Angels fly because they take themselves lightly

And so should we but we are so serious and sad, much of the time, as though we feel we 'should' be grown-up and cynical. But life is scary enough without us deliberately adding negativity to it. Why not believe in angels when you sense, however sceptical you try to be, that they not only exist but also are all around you? Doesn't it uplift you – just thinking of them? So think of your white feather often to remind you to go for that feeling, over and over again – when you need to or just because it's so good. They will lift you up with their wings and toss you into the air with joy and catch you like thistledown before setting you gently back to earth. Who knows – perhaps you will even learn to fly through life's problems!

How to use the symbol of the white feather when you are afraid

1 Think of how it would feel to have a little white feather resting in the palm of your hand, so light you can hardly feel it.
2 Let it remind you of your ability to speak and be listened to by the spiritual dimension and/or your inner personal power.
3 Ask for help. If you like, imagine shouting, 'Can I have some help, please!'
4 Wait for the help to come. Be aware so that, when it touches the reason for your fear, and in some way resolves and relieves it, you appreciate it.
5 Know that it may take time, and it may come in a way you hadn't thought of, but you will have help if you accept it and don't consciously block it with negative scepticism.

How to increase your spirituality

Although I've always appreciated the spiritual dimension and my moments of connection, it's taken me 53 years to realize something huge about it. I've been putting off writing this chapter, and then, deadline approaching, wrote the easy bit first – what could be nicer, once you face the 'I can't do it' fear and take the plunge, than writing about angels?

But spirituality generally . . . that's something else. So last night, meditating with friends, I acknowledged my fear again and asked: 'Which gift do I need?' and thought of the symbol of the white feather. I was already in that plane of mind where I was deeply relaxed so asking for help couldn't have been easier: 'Please . . . What do you want me to write?'

This is what I sensed:

Tell it like it is for you – your experience now, your experience over the years.

Most of all, tell about the joy of switching into the spiritual dimension of your being. Tell about the radiance you see and sense – in the atmosphere and shining from and around you and your friends. Say that it isn't anything weird and scary. It's bright and beautiful, feel-good, sparkly. It's deep communion with your great protector. It's sheer, unadulterated love. It's home. And it's there for you – for each and every one of you – whenever you remember to think of it.

A strange thing happened. Coming out of the meditation, my two friends and I looked at each other and we all registered the lightness and pleasure in each other's expressions. One by one we told of an unsurpassed experience of meditation or, more specifically, connection. Jane was thrilled as she said it was the first time she'd relaxed meditatively to that degree and had received some powerful personal insights. She glowed. Rita said she's been meditating for years but for the first time it had 'gone into her heart'. She positively beamed. I told them of the guidance I'd been given and the accompanying impression of the vibration of love and harmony filling the space around us and the feeling our individual auras had overlapped and joined together.

This was an especially good meditation. Often there are no revelations, nor even a faint sense of connecting with something else. Often you sit still and just quietly tune in without feeling you have done so. That's fine too. We don't have to expect a powerful connection or enlightenment, and just being still and 'being there' spiritually is at the same time relaxing and energizing.

Fears, acknowledged, settle into perspective

Whether you have an experience of communication or a quiet stillness, fears that come to mind can always be paid gentle attention, and told that the reasons for their warnings will be dealt with and allowed to fade out of our awareness. Then you can experience a healing space where you are washed through with love and the comforting understanding that all will be well.

Learning to meditate

I've tried transcendental meditation with a mantra, breathing exercises, yoga and all kinds of visualizations. All work for some people but not for everyone, and some people can slip into a meditative state using any of these methods or simply when they decide to. It's a very personal thing but, having tried them all, our group has found the easiest and quickest way in is simply to sit or kneel still, shut your eyes and compose yourself quietly, and breathe and exhale or sigh deeply a few times while imagining walking into a quiet place where you are happy and relaxed to be. And then continue to sit, very still, and hold your focus at the front of your head, in between your eyes or in the middle of your forehead. Whenever thoughts wander away, be aware of them and if they are fearful tell them you will pay attention to them later. Then let them go, gently returning your concentration to the focus again. Some people prefer to keep their eyes open and focus on the flame of a candle, and that's fine too.

If I don't have any pressing concerns and questions, I sit quietly, focusing and aware but letting myself slip into the centre of my body. At the same time I stay totally receptive should there be something I need to take in or become aware of. If I need help with a problem or anything I feel fearful about, I ask for help and then again rest quietly but receptive so I can pay full attention to any insights, understanding or answers that come to me.

How long to meditate? I'd recommend short sessions at first – perhaps just ten minutes. This is long enough to reach focus but short enough to stay there for the remaining time. As you practise – daily is great – you can then build up by five minutes every few times until you are comfortable meditating as long as you wish. For most of us this might be between half an hour and an hour but it is a very personal, individual choice. One very spiritual friend, Anete, rises at 5 a.m. every day to meditate for two hours before her active day begins. She is the wisest, most peaceful person I know.

Other ways to welcome and enhance your spirituality

(You may wish to skip this next bit if you're not a believer in God or a higher power, but I hope you don't because prayer is amazingly helpful in connecting with our potential and in restoring calm and positivity.)

Prayer is a direct connection and communion with God and more powerful than we can ever know. Like healing, it is both metaphysical and physical. When we *really* pray – not just saying the words but meaning them and really talking to God – we are in some way soothed, helped, healed and/or revitalized, as may be those for whom we pray.

How blessed our world will be when we all pray more!

And although of course it's lovely to talk with God when we're by ourselves, it's very moving to pray with another or others too. It's said the power of prayer is immeasurably intensified when two or more pray together for the same thing. We do this in our little group after meditating, and ask for healing for individuals we know who are ill and also for healing and help for troubled or war-torn areas.

Blow fears away

Pray and meditate regularly and always talk to God when you go out for a walk. I find it easiest when I'm in beautiful countryside or by the sea – somehow the open air, the light and the beauty combine to make the connection fluent and clear. For me and for many – including some of our greatest visionaries such as Wordsworth and Blake – spiritual experience, visions and a feeling of connection happen spontaneously and joyously in places like these.

The atmosphere in many churches can also be conducive to prayer and meditation. It's said that there is a special atmosphere in places where people have prayed and worshipped. Perhaps the love, prayer, celebration and worship experienced there have a physical effect. It may be that the style of the architecture and the nature and focus of our thoughts in such places is mood-enhancing. Whatever the reasons, if I'm feeling worn, weary or frightened for any reason, I'll sometimes go into a church and sit quietly for a while, letting the healing energy go to work. The white feather can remind you of such times in future and take you instantly into the calming state of mind you felt.

Neutralize fears

Connect, pray and meditate, and fears come naturally into perspective so we can deal with their cause effectively, with help from our angels, God and/or the healing energy that flows through us all the time if we allow it to.

The peace of God

Recognizing and nurturing a spiritual dimension in our lives develops a sense of deep calm and balance. Season it with praise, trust and love – of yourself and others – and this will reflect in everything you do and give you a wonderful sense of freedom that's not dependent on life going well.

Life will always have ups and downs, with fear trying to protect us from the downs and dangers. The gift of spiritual connection and your innate ability to love and protect yourself are symbolized by the white feather, which instantly reminds you to tune in to them. I believe we never have to face problems and troubles alone. I believe something other than us – God, a beneficial higher power, the universal energy of love, call it what you will – is always there for us. I believe angels look after us too, throughout our lives. I know from experience the more we connect and communicate, the more we let them help and follow their guidance, the easier life is. It follows that when we pass from this life to the next we'll have their help. No need for fear then; they will be with us to show us the way.

Reality or metaphors for our capacity (and deep human need) to feel protected? Either or both ways, we are much blessed.

6

A ripening seed:
use your creativity to dissolve fear

Think of a seed. Such a small thing and yet it has within it everything it needs to grow into and become the plant it is meant to be. And so have you, except that you are a multidimensional, thinking, feeling, highly intelligent being.

You are able to feel the whole gamut of human emotions but above all love and joy. You were designed with unique talents and to fulfil them will bring you peace and joy which will flow out to others. You have everything within your body, mind and soul that you need to live as fully and vibrantly as you were created to do.

Every seed has incredible energy and vitality. Just think of the power you have.

Think of the seed to help you grow
courageously towards your destiny

Think of the seed to inspire yourself, to grow and to know you can do whatever is right for you to do. So every time you need inspiration or question what love means or resent the fact you're not happy, every time you wonder what life is all about and what you are supposed to be doing here, think of your gift of a ripening seed. Imagine it sitting in your hand. So small yet so extraordinarily powerful and promising. You too have power and promise. You too will grow, given the right conditions. Essential to your development is your realization that you have the ability to grow towards your full potential. Isn't that the best, most awe-inspiring thing? You are a wonderful, totally unique being.

> Think of the seed whenever you doubt your ability and remember the amazing personal power a seed symbolizes: *your* personal potential and your ability to grow and live joyously.

You are a realm of possibility

So often we focus on fear of the future because we forget our talents and potential. Use the symbol of a seed to remind you how able you are to follow your best hopes and dreams. When you want something and feel it will be right for you, but find yourself standing back, terrified something will go wrong and it won't work, follow these steps:

1 Hold the seed in your hand and breath deeply and slowly, breathing in confidence and faith and breathing out fear and low self-esteem.
2 Think of what you want to do and achieve and how good it is.
3 Throw your heart out ahead of you, towards it, and then follow your heart.
4 Ask for courage and energy, like the seed, and take positive, practical steps to progress your idea.

Following this strategy gives projects their best chance of going through to fruition. But sometimes, of course, you'll find an idea doesn't work out despite your best efforts. One of the most creative men I know mentored me many years ago when he was my boss. I remember him saying, when I was devastated because an idea of mine that almost flew was suddenly grounded: 'Some of the best ideas are the ones we walk away from.' It's beautifully ambiguous, of course. It comforted me then because although I had been forced to let go of it, I was proud of my great idea even though it wasn't to be enacted. Another time a few years later his observation soothed me when I voluntarily walked away from an idea, only to see someone else pick it up and make millions with it. It happens.

At times like this, when an idea hasn't worked, imagine the seed and ask yourself for another. Your natural creativity will search and come up with all kinds of potential (see 'Further reading' on this). It's a strange thing, but so often when you let go of disappointment the new ideas that come turn out to be just as good. Different, but good and sometimes even better.

Face the fear whenever your self-esteem dips
and think of the seed to remind yourself of your
fundamental potential and ability to fulfil it

I have a dear friend who is a talented artist and produces work of uplifting beauty. But when she shows me something new, she says,

'It's no good. I'm not good at it. I can't do it.' And there, in her hand, is the proof that it is good, and she can do it.

We all try to convince her and make her see the truth, but fear blinds her or frightens her away from acknowledging and joying in her talent. 'You're making a fool of yourself if you think it's good,' it says to her. 'Call yourself an artist? Hah! Who are you to think you can paint? You have no talent.'

I hope that one day she will face her fears, look at their roots and pull them up. And if they grow again, as fears are prone to, that she will keep pulling them up, never letting them stifle her confidence again. It is not vain to acknowledge our gifts – it's common sense. They are there – why deny them? Of course we have to learn and practise, but if we are prepared to grow, put lots of energy and practise in and let our creativity flow, our work will improve. It is not foolhardy or arrogant to think we're good at something if we are, or to realize we can be if we work hard – it's a generous, polite response to our Creator or, if you prefer, our natural creativity. Also we all go through different stages and phases of our work as we learn anything and it is foolish to compare different levels. The beginner's work can be excellent but it is naturally different from the expert's. So face the fear of comparisons, think of the ripening seed and reassure yourself you are developing all the time.

You were born to relish your abilities. So slam down on fears that threaten your self-esteem. Most creative people (and that means everyone, one way or another) have them and we all need to face and rout them so they can no longer smother our creativity.

Hold the seed. Know that you too are growing, gathering wisdom, increasing your experience every day, maturing and stretching towards the light as the young plant stretches to face the sun.

When you recognize your creative ability and talent like this, fear subsides into perspective or disappears completely, for it is false.

Managing self-protective fears

Feel your energy

Take time to feel the life force within you. Notice what makes you feel motivated and gives you a sense of something good about to happen, inspiration in the air, a stirring, a beginning.

Remember the feeling and what caused it, and see if you can set up circumstances to repeat the inspiration. Seek it out; don't just wait for it to happen. But don't chase it – give it the opportunity and the freedom to appear if it will.

Give yourself space for it to happen and, when it does, give yourself time to pay attention to it. Plenty of time to be silent and think, or just be. To meditate, walk or relax quietly. To think about anything that comes into your head. Notice feelings and thoughts as they occur and see where they take you.

All this is food and light for your creativity

- Give yourself space and time and silence
- Let ideas and inspiration form if they try to
- Notice them
- Let the best grow – maybe straight, maybe shooting out in other directions
- Help it along
- Research
- Plan
- Get experience
- Nurture the idea
- Nurture your self
- Do what you can and see what happens
- If it looks as though it's going to be good, follow it through
- Feel the sparkle, feel the joy and satisfaction

Pay special attention to this last point. One of the most common reasons for dreams and good ideas not to become reality is they're not followed through. Fears set in and what could have become something good is allowed to wither.

Instead:

- look at each fear;
- see the point it's making;
- deal with it.

If you see clearly that the risk of a project is too great or is in some way not right for you after all, then shelve it. Then you can leave it behind, knowing you've done the right thing, not fearful that you shouldn't have given up and/or were too quick to. Thank the fear for its protective warning and pay attention to logic and gut feeling. If both tell you it's right to continue, do so – you already have confidence and courage.

You are designed to develop . . .

It's easy to be so daunted by life that we stunt our own growth. Think of the seed if you are frightened that you or your ideas aren't going to come to anything. Give yourself tender loving care, including the right conditions for growth, and you *will* grow – nothing is more certain because your potential is inbuilt.

Turn fear into love. Love yourself tenderly, compassionately. Be realistic, but be optimistic too. Love your projects passionately. And appreciate it to the full when you find yourself moving effortlessly towards your goal.

. . . And to flow

Most artists know the feeling when their work suddenly stops being a conscious, thinking effort. Suddenly your body is making the moves of its own volition to put paint on canvas, dance, make music, write or create whatever else you are creating. It's as though a flow of creativity is directed through you. You are an instrument being beautifully played.

You know this can happen. You've experienced it or sense you could experience it. So you know you have what it takes. Think of the seed to help. Ask for this shift of energy, this catharsis to happen. And whenever a creative phase has flowed through you, delight in the sense of fruition and satisfaction and give thanks.

It's all about love. Remember, love is the opposite of fear. Love yourself, your work and the energy that drives our world and you will smile on your creativity and breathe it into life.

When you're following your genuine interests you'll be interested and interesting. Your self-esteem will start to grow; it feels good to do your own thing and think creatively and as you start to shine so will your whole life. This builds a strong base and you'll feel stronger and more capable.

Fear will be your ally

Fear, in this climate of growth and confidence, will still touch you on the shoulder sometimes to warn you of unseen or ignored dangers, but you'll feel much better equipped to face it and deal with what it's telling you. This way fear won't settle in and bother you on an ongoing basis. When you're expressing yourself through your interests, skills and talents, you'll be living and thinking creatively. It feels great.

Practise, practise, practise. Once again, it's so easy not to do something we really want to do. So deal constructively with obstructions:

- 'I haven't got time.' Make time, even just five minutes at a time at first. Make this a priority.
- 'I'm no good.' You have the ability to get good. Trying is the first step to success. If you don't try, you'll never see how good you can be.

This is your life. Your extraordinary mind. Your beautiful body. Your myriad gifts and abilities. Use them *now*. We none of us know for definite what's going to happen tomorrow but we do have our present in our hands to do with what we will.

- Don't let the sun go down on a day when you haven't thought or done something new or creative.
- Go for it, full on – no one else can use your life for you.
- Turn off the television or the computer and relish your time, your possibility.

Maximize your energy, your time, your creativity, your sheer, amazing ability and you will live in freedom and fulfilment.

7

A pair of skates:
glide through life smoothly and safely

Sometimes life just seems thoroughly difficult. Nothing happens to plan, things go wrong – or aren't quite right. You find yourself taking wrong turnings, literally and metaphorically, and having to retrace your steps, wasting more time and energy. You worry that at this rate you'll only complete a fraction of what you're meant to accomplish. Your progress, in other words, is out of control and you don't like it.

So you are scared – because life isn't going how you thought it would and think it should. And the fear, grinding away at your soul, makes you falter even more, or procrastinate or frantically take new wrong directions which lead you deeper into that feeling of being incompetent – or lost.

Transform the situation

Your skates are for the times when the path is too rough or the going too heavy – a strong inspiration to transform the discomfort of this scenario. They stand for your ability to travel smoothly through life. No more struggling. You have or can learn the skills required for any terrain. Life isn't always easy but you will always get through and needn't ever lapse into panic.

Success isn't about struggle. There will be work but, rather than *hard* slog, think of it as work gladly given. Your choice, thoroughly enjoyed, with fulfilment in the doing as well as the achievement at the end of the day.

Enjoying your purpose each day, be it work or leisure, is like skating. You glide through it with easy steps, stroking the ground you cover not effortlessly but pleasurably, full of energy to power you, smoothing the way as you go.

Ride changes easily by changing the way you move

So often we get snagged on changes. It's frightening being held back or even stopped in our tracks, even if we won't admit it. And if we don't embrace the fear, learn from it and let it transmute into courage we'll complain about every bit of uneven ground. I bet you know someone who is always moaning about their life and their lot. Don't you find yourself doing it too, at least sometimes? Grumbling is made of fear and it makes more fear.

But face the fear and you can swing into a forward movement that's graceful and sure, and some of the way will be an amazing, fun-filled dance.

Suss out the fear

Probably it's there to protect you. So *hug it!* Listen to what it wants to tell you. Get all the information you need – research, think, take advice, listen to your gut feeling. Fear? No longer – now your courage is equipped and ready to take off on the next stage of your life. That could mean no change at the moment – or yes, go for it. Think of the skates. Imagine yourself skating – gliding along, swooshing – the best feeling: harmony and movement, coordination and smoothness.

What if you need to let go and move on, but are stalled?

Sometimes we get stuck in situations because there's a lot we like about them and it's hard to say goodbye to that. You're scared of having to face and feel the grief you know will overcome you when you do let go and walk away. Or you can be seriously hooked and held by a habit – that's really tough, too. It's seriously frightening to think of quitting something you're so used to. It's part of your life, even when it's hurting you. Addicted to pain? Plenty of people are. As with depression or even abuse from a partner – you can learn to depend on it.

But you have the ability to let go of the psychological bond and move on. First be aware of it. Once familiar with it, you can say, as to a friend, 'Thank you – I understand where you're coming from but I can manage on my own now.'

The symbol of the skates will help. Just imagine holding them in your hands. Aren't they something? Now put them on and feel how it will be – see yourself, hear the sound – as you make your first moves, one flowing into the next, establishing pace, building momentum, slowing as you want, stopping when you decide. Your moves, your call, your ability to move through life in the manner you wish – confidently and with your own unique, beautiful style.

1 You have the ability to move through life smoothly and gracefully and choosing your pace. Hold the skates in your hand and remember what they mean.
2 Believe this. Repeat it to yourself whenever you feel you're making a mess of something.
3 Review the last and current phases of your journey. Why the mistakes or ineptitude?
4 Are you on the right road for you? (If not, check out your map.)
5 If yes, then you have the inbuilt ability to follow it.
6 What do you need to make it possible? Research? Practice? Advice? Go and get it.
7 Tell your fear you have the ability you need and are doing what you need to maximize it.
8 Ask for courage – it will flow into the space left by fear as you send it packing.
9 Imagine wearing your life skates. From now on move confidently, with poise, calmly but powerfully.
10 You have tremendous personal power. Know it. Feel it. Use it.

Why are you procrastinating about something you want to do?

You've guessed it. Because you're fearful.

Procrastination is such a waste of time. I know all about it – give me half a chance and I'll dither. Mostly it's because we fear either that we'll make the wrong decision or we'll make the right one and then be hopeless and mess it up. There's another fear: that our effort will be scorned or rejected.

As you read this, you are probably already aware of the personal fears that keep you fidgeting and frustrated, rooted to the spot. (If not, take a while to look into it.) The fears are doing their usual job, trying to protect you. But you need to be very firm with them. What are they telling you? OK – heed the warning. If you still want to go ahead, what do you need to do to lessen the chances of messing up and/or being rejected? Do it. Thoroughly, conscientiously to the best of your ability. You know you can. Think of the skates to remind you. Move confidently, steadily, in your own unique style, sweeping smoothly forward towards your goal.

If, on the other hand, you face the fear and see it has a definite point, think it through once more. If the risks outweigh the potential, don't do it. But think carefully. If you believe you could do it well, and it would be good for you if it works out, don't let the possibility of rejection deter you. The world's most successful people all take risks. Most of them suffer many setbacks, rejections and failures. They realize the ongoing flow of inner happiness and spirit is not about achievement but about being in flow – skating rhythmically towards and through the things you want, hope, need and love to do.

You can do this too. You have the ability. If you fall (even the best skaters fall over sometimes) you pick yourself up and get going again, evaluating the best way forward. Do you continue towards the goal or rethink and, if necessary, regroup and set off towards another more feasible one? Learn from your mistakes and from others, and don't let them faze you. Like fear, they are there to deepen your experience and teach you.

The melting pot of experience

Every single thing that happens to us in this life goes into the melting pot of experience. Even negative experiences that scare you stiff grow your soul if you refuse to hide, face them and learn. It does take courage. But as you turn to face fear so courage swings in behind you, holding you up. Fear gives you its message and disappears as you and courage prepare to skate on.

Life is a dance – skating makes it easier, the pace faster (if you wish). Skating through life is rhythmic, harmonious, coordinated. And fun.

Why skates?

Because the image of a good skater is easy to visualize and everything about skating symbolizes the beautiful, coordinated way we can all go through life if we take the right attitude and believe in ourselves.

Are you old enough to remember the skaters Torvill and Dean? Their performances took the nation's breath away with their beauty and harmony of movement. And there was a spiritual element – their skating touched souls as we watched, spellbound.

Follow your dream

Those young skaters followed their dream. They both learned to skate, practised and practised and loved it with a passion. They dreamt of going to the top and skated all the way there.

You can live your life this way, following your dream of how it can be. Bring the image of your skates to mind whenever you need inspiration or think you may fall. Skate on: you have the ability and the grace to achieve your potential and – most important of all – to enjoy the journey.

- Have a dream you can move towards
- Skate away on the path – every journey begins with a first step
- Get in a rhythm
- Feel the momentum, the energy
- Thrill to the exhilaration of going where you want to go

The skates are a metaphor for your ability to get in motion, go with the flow, find coordination and follow your dreams through your life. Harmony; energy; forward, decisive, precise motion; control; fluidity; flow. You have it all. It's your gift. Use it to live life the way you want. You'll light up your loved ones and all you meet along the way with your joy.

Skates:
Glide on through things. Get up pace. The steps you take, the moves you make facilitate your forward thrust or gentle momentum. Make it positive, make it smooth. Every move focused but relaxed. Dancing with life, dancing through life in harmony.

Getting on with people

When relationship fears strike or nag, the skates will also remind you of your power to live your relationships with others gracefully, positively and kindly. Is someone rubbing you up the wrong way or are you conscious, if you're honest, that you're needling someone else? Heed the language. 'Rubbing', 'needling' – it feels horrible, doesn't it? Snaggy and rough, just like the way you both feel when you get caught up in each other's scaly crossness. This is what you do:

1 Feel the roughness of the atmosphere between you.
2 Decide you want to improve it – smooth the scratchiness, iron out lumpy disagreements.
3 Keeping these visual impressions of your prickly interaction in mind, think of ways to change the picture.
4 Think of a crystal as well (see Chapter 11). Imagine the air around you and between you being ionized with positivity instead of the existing negativity.
5 Think of how you could actually like aspects of this person instead of focusing on all the things that rub you up the wrong way.
6 Be curious to see how changing your attitude and behaviour towards them to something positive, genuinely helpful and thoughtful can change their behaviour towards you.
7 Now go for it. Give it your best. Think of the skates: think of yourself smoothing the way so you can both travel forwards gracefully, with dignity and, if not exactly a rapport (though that may come!) at least mutual tolerance and respect.

I promise you – life is so much easier and pleasurable if we get on with people, or just let them get on with their own negativity if they're stuck in it, instead of getting up against them. Remember, no matter how someone else is behaving, you have the ability to behave gracefully and kindly. Skate on! You don't have to falter in the ground they're trying to make uneven. Be aware of the fear, face it, thank it, but tell it firmly you can stay balanced, fluent, unruffled.

Skaters cover the ground and dance through the air in a poetry of motion. Think of your skates and all they symbolize and get in touch with your ability to be graceful in all you do and in your contact with others. It feels so good!

8

A healing elixir: drink in a new attitude to heal your life

Good health is such a delight. When our bodies are on top form we feel good in ourselves too – it's easy to laugh and dance and love and enjoy life generally when we're well. But sometimes, even when we're well, we can get scared we won't always be and of course illness itself makes us fearful. Fears like this are distressing so we may ignore them, but this isn't a good idea.

For the fear has a purpose: it's knocking, knocking, knocking – persistently urging us to open up to its message of love. It wants to remind us we can do a lot to look after our health and avoid illness and that we have astonishing self-healing power, plus the ability to manage illness and seek out and hopefully resolve contributory factors. We also have the ability to access others' expertise and healing. Once we take our illness in hand ourselves like this, fear largely disappears.

I use the symbol of an elixir to help call on these innate gifts whenever healing is needed or energy levels can do with a lift. When the image of a little bottle containing an elixir of healing fluid was given to me in a meditation, I remembered the story of how Lucy is given a similar elixir in C. S. Lewis's *Chronicles of Narnia*. Sometimes she is paralysed with fear of her powerlessness in the face of suffering but when she remembers her gift she is galvanized into action, healing and saving lives. We all have this gift to some extent but, like Lucy, we often forget to use it. Remembering, and imagining giving the elixir to others and absorbing it ourselves, we are instantly reminded of the healing energy that surges into action immediately we ask for its help.

When science and spirituality work together, in some way emotional or physical healing commences or intensifies, and fear fades. Many doctors now believe that focused healing by a healer or by yourself can have a positive emotional and physical effect. This may be completely or to some extent a psychosomatic effect, with the relieving thought 'we are being healed' releasing health-promoting factors such as 'feel-good' endorphins, and also helping to adjust the levels of various nerve-message chemicals (neurotransmitters such as adrenaline and serotonin) and boosting the efficiency of the immune system.

Like many who heal or have been healed in some way, I believe that focused healing may also have powerful energy in its own right that helps the above responses. But, as with all the symbols in this book, you don't have to believe this to make use of this gift and nothing that I say here should deter you from seeking appropriate medical advice when you're unwell.

The healing elixir is a powerful symbol to remind us of our own and others' healing power.

How to use it

Imagine:

1 Holding in your hand a little bottle containing a liquid which is an elixir of healing power. Visualize it, feel it – a small bottle.
2 Tilt it to your lips and let a couple of drops of the precious, healing fluid fall onto your tongue. You may find it helpful to mime this.
3 Feel the liquid in your mouth and swallow it.
4 Sense its healing power as it is absorbed by your body.
5 Feel your worries and fears being calmed by the elixir as its healing energy sweeps through you.

Do this whenever you feel you need healing. Whatever the ailment or health worry that prompts you to ask the elixir's help, you will feel calmer. Because you feel better, quite naturally you will actually be healed in some way, even if only of some anxiety.

How does it work?

One of the explanations for real healing after a visualization like this is that when we think healing, calming thoughts, it triggers the physiological changes already mentioned above, so:

- Our heart rate slows, helping us feel less panicky.
- Our production of painkilling, soothing endorphins rises; these are natural hormone-like opiates that help us relax and feel better. It isn't just imagination – it actually happens.

- When we are ill we are usually frightened, and in response our adrenal glands pump adrenaline into our bloodstream and our sympathetic nervous system prepares our body for fight or flight. This stress response makes our heart beat faster and we may hyperventilate (breathe faster and more shallowly); also, we perspire, our blood pressure rises, and our digestion slows or stops. Another emergency measure, and one which can become prolonged, is the release into the body's tissues of histamines – the sort of prostaglandins (hormone-like chemicals) that encourage inflammation – and immune cells (from the bloodstream). All this would be very helpful if we were about to be knifed, but it's bad news if it's continued due to long term fear, as it reduces immunity and encourages auto-immune diseases such as rheumatoid arthritis to develop. But healing thoughts and relaxation that calm us and release us from fear enable our parasympathetic nervous system to reverse the stress response; our heart rate and blood pressure then decrease and our digestive and immune systems start working properly again.

Interestingly, I've noticed that visualizing the elixir makes my mind more alert, if I need to be, or drowsy if I want to relax completely and go to sleep. Does that sound unlikely? Hardly – our minds are far brighter and more sensitive than we used to think they were. They want to help us and, given the chance, they do.

The elixir is a precious friend that encourages you to be aware of your own and others' healing power, and to welcome it and let it stream through you. Healing thoughts encourage a calming process that may encourage cell renewal and improve the immune system. At the very least they make you feel better and diminish pain, or help you manage pain less stressfully.

Keeping going when your heart is broken

The elixir is also a symbol of the support you can summon from within when immersed in grief and the fear that accompanies the loss when a loved one dies. This is not the place to go fully and deeply into coping with a bereavement, but thinking of the elixir puts you in touch with your innate strength and healing power, which will help you cope with this immense emotional trauma.

Courage comes when we remember that love is never wasted and can endure. You can continue to think of the person, imagine them with you, talk to them. You can remember so many shared experiences and, in giving thanks, find some relief and help the healing process, which – hard though it may be to believe it – has begun and will in time ease the pain.

Ranulph Fiennes told me of his tremendous grief following the death of his wife. They had known each other since childhood and were married for 35 years. He spoke of three things that help him cope without her:

> I think how incredibly lucky I am to have lived for so many years with the best person in the world and I thank God that I was able to be with her during her illness to help her. I also work as hard as possible. I am constantly on the move.

Everyone's experience of grief after the loss of someone greatly loved is unique, but remembrance of the love shared is a beacon of light to help us through. Happy memories, positively chosen, give joy even in the midst of sorrow and help heal the agony of loss. Work and other physical and mental activity are also helpful on two fronts: they give you valuable respite from the sadness for short periods allowing rest, and they release 'feel-good' hormones, such as endorphins and serotonin, which may make the grief more bearable.

A practical plan for everyday healing and health

I met a friend today who was recently taken seriously ill and is only just recovering. He said the illness had taken him by surprise and continues to frighten him as he'd never been ill before. It knocked him sideways – one day fit and well, the next facing chronic pain and the possibility of impending death.

For him, as for most people, the idea of serious illness befalling him, and even death, which after all is inevitable one day, had previously been a no-go zone in his thinking. The prospect is just too frightening to contemplate.

But is it? I haven't experienced chronic pain but I have just made the acquaintance of a new friend, Audrey, who lives with it and with the likelihood it will get worse as time goes by. She is remarkably cheerful and clearly leads a fulfilling life. If anyone appears to have the gift of an elixir to help her manage her illness, she does. Talking to her is like a tonic – perhaps she is herself an elixir of health?

The healing power of positive thinking

When I first met Audrey, even as she extricated herself from the car, I sensed her calm, confident spirit. Although it was a difficult and slow manoeuvre as she has severe, chronic osteoarthritis, she neither requested nor accepted offers of help. Quietly determined, she wanted to do it herself. 'For as long as I can I want to keep my independence,' she later told me.

Going into the house my dog and two cats were clearly interested in her and eager to make her acquaintance and talk to her. This was especially unusual for the little tabby who was recovering from an ear operation and had been lying very low until then, scarcely talking to me let alone strangers. Audrey was the first person she'd taken an express interest in.

Later I said to Audrey: 'You talk to them, don't you?'

'Oh yes,' she said. 'I always talk to animals.'

Later, when I began writing this book, I asked her how she dealt with fears about her encroaching illness. She said she would think about it and come back to me. This is what she wrote:

After pondering hard I have come to these conclusions and hope they may help someone.

- Acceptance – decisions – exercise.
- Each morning on arising and each evening on retiring gently manipulate (massage and move) every joint. From your jaw through to your fingertips and waist down to your toe tips – eight bends on each joint. Keep mobile!
- Keep your self-respect with regard to personal hygiene, using cutlery and feeding yourself and also in dressing, etc. If necessary use a stick or one of the many gadgets available to assist.
- Do not sit around bemoaning the fact you're disabled and/or in pain.
- Improve your knowledge by reading, or take an interest in the house, greenhouse, pot plants and sewing if possible.
- Keep walking as long as possible – take short, gentle steps.

There are many things you can do to take your mind away from the pain. Try it – it works for me.

And always remember, laughter is a great help – tears only worsen the problem. Fight, fight, fight! Tell yourself it won't defeat you.

Remember pain develops from the mind, and the old saying, 'mind over matter', can ease pain although it won't cure it.

Avoid involving others in discussions about your disability. They cannot fully understand unless they too have experienced pain. Always give them the impression you are fine. It will make *you* feel better because the conversation will be more exhilarating and refreshing.

In summary: acceptance – decision – determination – fight – laughter – no tears

Footnote

After taking prescription drugs for almost 13 years I have now turned to herbal medicine and find much benefit. The decision was taken because the prescription drugs were giving me no real relief, and the complication of suffering the consequences of, in some instances, lethal side effects, made the gentleness of using herbal products an easy choice. I wish I had decided to do this earlier. I would also be more assertive to make sure I was not pushed to one side by doctors who have little time for chronic illness.

Sometimes, like Audrey, we may not be able to be physically cured but we will always receive healing in some form – mind, body or spirit – if we invite and allow it. The symbol of the healing elixir is a reminder to do this.

It's also a reminder that life can be good even when we are incapacitated. For example and inspiration, we only have to look to those who are, or have been, paralysed or severely disabled – notably the late Christopher Reeve and Dr Steven Hawking. In my local town I think of two women, both paraplegic after accidents. All nonetheless continue to live extremely useful lives joyfully. There will be others like them local to you.

Think of the elixir and its message of your own self-healing body and mind, and your ability to self-manage the way you cope with illness and incapacity.

And as for fear of death

Like all the other fears, listen to it and do what it's asking you. Perhaps you need to accept you're going to die one day and to think about how to do so as peacefully and mindfully as possible. Is this important? Absolutely. Those who regularly help the dying know death can be approached in many ways and feel that doing so gracefully, lovingly and acceptingly eases the passage from this life to the next.

And talking about it eradicates fear. I first found this out by chance as a small child. I asked my father what it meant, where we'd go, what would it be like and so on and of course he didn't have the answers. I thought about it for quite a long while and came to this conclusion, which I still think is as far as we can get for certain. If our souls do live on when our bodies die, then it's going to be a huge adventure. But if there is no next life, which I can't believe but have to acknowledge is possible, then it will simply be like going to sleep, or maybe having an anaesthetic. Lights out and eternal peace.

Either way it seems to me death is nothing to be frightened of.

But however philosophical we are, sometimes fear of our mortality bubbles up again. Think of the elixir and of the ability you have which it symbolizes – to manage your health as you live, and be aware that, when the time comes, we can take a peaceful approach to death too.

Living well – taking the elixir every day

Our bodies and minds are so precious that it makes sense to look after ourselves as well as we possibly can. Taking a quick look at the elixir every day or at least once a week reminds us to live well, giving us the best possible chance to enjoy our health.

We need to pay attention to it because good health doesn't happen automatically, it's a direct result of how we live. Taking an all-round perspective we can look after our bodies and help our natural healing processes work well. You don't have to be a health fanatic – remembering some basic principles is all it takes.

- Eat a varied diet based on natural foods. Try to make sure your daily diet includes fruit, leafy green vegetables and/or salads and some natural (i.e. not salted or roasted) nuts and seeds. Include some whole carbohydrate such as pulses, potatoes and wholemeal bread, but go steady on these. Have plenty of protein – choose from eggs, yoghurt, nuts, pulses, cheese, tofu; or meat, poultry (always free range), or fish. Buy organic foods as much as possible to save your body having to cope with the effects of chemicals used in production. And if you eat meat make sure it comes from local farms where the animals are well cared for and not transported alive on long journeys.

- Drink plenty of water and minimal amounts of sugary or chemical-enriched soft drinks. If you like coffee and tea, drink it very weak or limit yourself to only one strong cup a day and, if you want to sleep well at night, don't drink it after say 2 p.m.
- Savour everything you eat – taking your time to taste and enjoy each mouthful. In lingering over meals, we give our bodies and minds a chance to realize when our appetite is satisfied, and chewing food well helps digestion and natural metabolism.
- Get out in the light every day for at least half an hour (taking care not to burn).
- Exercise every day – walking or swimming is fine.

For more detailed advice, see 'Further reading'.

Feel good about yourself. You are a unique person with an amazing body. A double gift! Enjoy life, enjoy being you – body, mind and soul, and enjoy feeding and looking after yourself well and healthily. We are so fortunate to be able to do so. Give thanks for your life, every single day.

9

A pen and ink:
write fear out of your day

You are the author of your life and the pen and ink symbolizes your amazing ability to write your script. Each day and all the moments – this very time now – is yours to live as you decide to live it. What you do, how you are, how you relate to others and your attitude to everyone and everything around you is your story.

Whenever you are flummoxed by something and panic, 'I can't do this', call to mind your gift of a pen and ink and remember you have your own internal life-writing equipment – you just need to use it.

Say this to yourself, out loud if possible: 'Whatever life presents me with, I can deal with.'

It doesn't mean no effort – often we need to put lots of attention and energy into what we want to do – but once you action your ability to write and follow your own script, the inspiration and ideas to get you going will arrive. You'll find yourself able to work on the situation, doing what you need to do – getting help when necessary – and step by step working through it.

What fears do the pen and ink apply to?

The pen and ink represents potently our innate power to assess and lay to rest the common fears that:

- We're not getting our lives right and are wasting the precious moments and years;
- We can't make others understand us or even listen to us;
- We have no talent, or what we do have is worthless;
- We are worthless;
- Confusion and chaos will overwhelm us;
- We sail on the surface of life with no rudder, life jacket or anchor.

You have the ability to deal with all these fears

It's there for you to harness whenever you are scared you can't do something or can't communicate with others. The pen and ink represents your ability:

- To write your own story and let it develop the right way;
- To communicate with others calmly and confidently;
- To be creative according to your aptitude, talents and skills – writing, painting, dancing, music making or crafting – you have the ability and the energy;
- To think creatively through situations, making sense of all the issues and aspects and suggesting possible changes;
- To freeflow write, allowing your subconscious understanding to let your truth clarify things for you and heal hurt.

Your story

Think of your gift of a pen and ink to help you write your own life script and become the best you can be. You will instantly sense your own ability to live well, with help available to you whenever you recognize your need and ask for help.

Use your inner power to live your life the best way you can and to help others live well too. You can have a dynamic effect on others – those closest to you at home and at work, and, in a ripple effect, people all over the world. Don't underestimate your potential for good – it is greater than you have ever dreamed.

Henri Matisse said, 'The essential thing is to say well what you have to say.' He spoke in the context of his great talent – painting – but it applies to every expression of ourselves. With this intention in mind, the making of your life story will be pleasurable and the tale that unfolds day by day – your life – will be fulfilling and often beautiful.

> Your affirmation: 'I can and I will do my best.'

'But no one can be happy and get it right all the time, can they?'

No, it's not possible of course, for over the years even those with the supposedly most charmed lives will have to face adverse circumstances and sorrows. But all adversity presents challenges and experiences, maturing and enriching our lives in some way and giving valuable perspective. Someone once pulled me out of a 'poor me' fit of depression by saying, 'If you didn't know the downs, you couldn't appreciate the ups.' It's true. If everything were always perfect it wouldn't seem perfect any more because we'd have nothing to gauge the feeling against and, anyway, it might even get boring. Others' actions and interactions with us, sheer fate and our own misguided choices mean life is a mixture of experiences. Each in some way is of value to you. So recognize each – even fear and its reasons – as part of your story, somehow enriching it or teaching you something. See the dramas and the lulls, but always keep the narrative in mind – it's your lifeline, your life blood as you journey through your lifetime in this world.

Your creativity

I talk to so many people who insist they are not creative, and many others who know they are, but constantly undervalue their talent and, in so doing, themselves. We are all creative, we all have worthwhile ability and denying it triggers an invidious fear that we are missing something and fosters low self-esteem. However apparently success-ful our lives, there is so often this feeling of deep, scarcely recognized unease.

The fact is most of us need to be creative. Is this striking a chord – either making you say 'Yes – that's so true of me' or else feeling distinctly irritating? Either way believe it – you *are* a creative person and if you're feeling angry as you read this it probably indicates you're not letting your creativity flow, or at least not often enough.

So use the pen and ink as a symbol to remind you, and practically as a tool, to get in flow. Write and write and write. Write your heart out. It doesn't matter what you write. Let the words drop in sequence onto the paper or screen, even if they seem meaningless, for they will flush away the block and let your creativity begin to come through. It may be a trickle, it may come with a whoosh of power and joy – but start it will to flow.

Or, if you're not a words person, draw or paint. Maybe use a pencil – a lovely fat soft one – instead of a pen. Or use a brush or palette knife and paint. Or gorgeous chunky soft pastels – whatever medium appeals.

Fear disappears when you get in flow and let your mind communicate what it will onto paper or screen, board or canvas.

Dance works the same way too: put on some music you love –
anything as long as you absolutely adore it. For if it moves you
emotionally it will move you physically and in dancing – slowly,
softly, sensuously or wild, powerfully, erotically; whatever is right
for you in the moment – your creativity dances too and fear doesn't
stand a chance.

Whatever your kind of creativity, the unblocking principle is the
same. Just do it – make what you want to make, practise your craft,
sing, make music, design, engineer, cook, garden. Whatever you
engage in, let your creativity guide you and come through.

Oust the 'I'm not creative' fear on a daily basis

While spontaneous bouts of pen pushing, painting or dancing can
work wonders on that insidiously scary blocked feeling, a gentler,
regular practise on a daily basis is even better. Start your day with a
15-minute session – that's all it takes – and you'll feel you can
breathe deeper and easier throughout the rest of the day, look
everyone you meet in the eye and not be panicked by anyone or
anything.

I don't know how it banishes fear, I just know that it does. Isn't it
fantastic – that something so simple, that takes so little time, can
have such an impact on your life? And as well as unplugging your
talent, it builds it. Practice may not make perfect but it certainly
improves.

Don't let it elude you

There is a snag. Daily writing practice is as elusive as can be. It slips
away from you. You wake up and forget it completely. Or you think,
'After my bath/breakfast/getting the children up' or 'Sod it! I'm not
doing it today.'

I beg you not to let it get away from you. Demand control of
yourself. If you must, cut it to ten or even five minutes, but do that
thing that makes you feel better – put words on paper, or paint, or
dance.

Like most things, once you establish a habit it becomes easier but,
unlike bad habits, it won't grab you by the throat and make you
addicted. You have to grab it by the throat and love it, live by it,
celebrate it. 'Yes! I am going to do this and that's that.'

Can't or won't? Maybe you like your fear then? Can that be true? No – not this kind of fear. It's debilitating to wake up feeling uneasy, unfulfilled and incomplete. So use the thought of your gift, the pen and ink, to spur you into action.

Who knows? It may do more than unblock you and rout your fear in the process. With the inspiration and regular practice of the daily flow session, you could become so great at what you're doing that you take off into a new career.

If so – invite me to the launch party, private view or first night, please – you'll recognize me by the little pen-and-ink charm on my necklace.

Writing your way through fears to confidence and clarity

Journal writing is a calming, confidence-giving practice. Writing about what's going on in your life right now helps soothe and balance fears and worries so you're well-placed to deal with the reasons. Aim for a daily entry, but don't worry if days or weeks go by – get going again and the benefits will still be there for you. The joy of a journal is its emphasis on your personal impressions – let them pour onto the page as they come to you, describing your feelings about each scene you remember and the situation as a whole.

Letters are great too, both e- and snail mail. In a personal letter you can ramble as you think. For business letters you need to keep to the point and that concentrates the mind.

Writing your thoughts pins them down – there they are, in front of you in black and white. Now you can get them into order and make sense of them. Think of your thoughts tumbling as words onto the page, willing messengers of facts and feelings.

Aim to focus, flow, shed light and yet have a light touch, and your letters will shine – brightening up the recipient's moment as they read and potentially clarifying their thoughts too.

Communicate – you have a natural ability

'They don't understand. I can't make myself clear. They don't want to listen. No one hears what I say. No one takes any notice of what I think.' Does this sound familiar? Then use the pen and ink symbol to focus your mind on the fact that you can be clear, people will listen and hear what you say and they will take notice.

Start by clarifying your thoughts in your own mind first. You won't get and hold attention if you have nothing to say or it comes out muddled. Either write your thoughts down or, when you're with other people and don't have the chance, think through the main points you want to make. The image of the pen and ink will help you remember to do this and this affirmation will help your words flow: 'I have something relevant and interesting to say and will speak clearly and compellingly.'

In general, building your self-esteem and assertiveness will help you develop a sense of presence which everyone will notice and be pleased by – it's so much easier for others when we speak audibly and positively.

Think, too, of helping others deal with their own fears – even the most seemingly confident of people often fear people aren't listening to them. So be a great listener as well as a talker and then, when you speak, they will return the compliment and pay attention to you.

Affirmation: I am a good communicator and can write a good letter.

Think of the pen and imagine that the ink flowing from it is confidence in your ability to do what you want to do. You can manage this moment, this phase of your life. You can communicate fluently. You are your own personal story teller and the way you live your story and write your days will be good.

10

A light: light up your life and banish the darkness of fear and depression

Any kind of confusion, darkness, fog or depression can be scary. And many kinds of fear make us feel confused or lost. So the darkness of fear can be a vicious cycle. Most of us have times when we long for some light, sensing it will help us halt the circle and chase away our unease. And light is there for us whenever we need it, for we have the inborn power to light up our darkness and lighten our lives.

The light is a potent symbol of your ability to shine light on anything that needs illuminating. Even the darkest situations can be lit up. It's also about health – light is life-giving and healing, and we need to absorb some each day. Life is transformed when we live in the light and again it's our choice to, every day.

Using the light

Usually when light's needed you will long for it – for we reach naturally towards light just as plants do, turning our faces towards it and soaking it up, or directing it onto whatever needs enlightening. But when we're busy, stressed, not well or fearful for any reason, we sometimes find ourselves lacking light in one sense or another, often without realizing it.

1 When you ask in your mind for a gift to help you and a source of light comes to mind, be aware of the form it takes for you. I visualize a lantern but you may see a torch, a bright candle or another kind of light.
2 Sense its meaning. Listen for what it tells you of your ability to shed light around you or where it's needed.
3 Think of ways to do this.
4 Does it mean anything else to you?
5 Now imagine light flooding around you, beaming into you, warming you, lightening your heart and giving you energy.
6 Think of the energy and speed of light. Your healing power and love also have the potential to touch someone else, thousands

of miles away, shining light for them as well as for you. Send your light out into the world now and often in thought, communication and kind gestures.

How to turn the light back on when depression darkens your life

Depression is a scourge of modern society. We've never had it better and yet that in itself puts us under pressure – we think we ought to be happy and are fearful if we're not or, when we are, are scared it won't last. Unacknowledged fear can lead to depression and is always a part of it. Most of us know what it's like to feel depressed, which means we know fear and need to know how to deal with it. Think of depression and you'll be aware of something very physical. There's a sense of darkness and it isn't just an analogy – when you are depressed it's actually as though the lights have been dimmed. I've experienced it as a time of misty greyness, even when the sun was shining bright. Others describe the darkening as blue or black – hence 'a fit of the blues' and Churchill's 'black dog'. There may also be the physical sensation of being weighted, pushed or pulled down.

It's very, very frightening. If it hasn't happened to you before you may wonder if you're going mad and/or whether you'll ever get back to your normal happy or at least happier self. Everything you do is more of an effort. You want to hide away but if you do that you may be more frightened than ever.

If you've been depressed for more than a few days, it's important to see your doctor. Whether it's a natural and transitory response to circumstances, or a chemical imbalance in the brain or a mixture of both, it may benefit from the medical treatment and/or the counselling your GP can organize. Alongside your doctor's advice and treatment, you might find the following helpful.

Your ability to light up the darkness and lighten the load

Normally there is a huge amount we can do ourselves to alleviate, resolve or eliminate causes and enable the healing process so we come safely through the depression. The light is a therapeutic symbol of your natural self-healing ability.

To inspire you, do this healing visualization every day until the light breaks through completely and your depression lifts:

1 Breathe slowly and deeply for a while as you relax. Focus on your breathing, and then on de-tensing every part of your body from toe to head.
2 Now imagine a very beautiful, pure light beaming down on you and flooding you with light.
3 Feel it lightening your spirit and bathing your heart with joy and love.
4 Ask it to heal your sadness, dispel fear and give you courage and the resources to cope with difficulties.
5 Imagine it recharging your own source of light and love and know that it will automatically replenish itself from now on.
6 Now direct a beam of light onto any situation that needs clarifying.
7 Ask for enlightenment and understanding.
8 Now be still a while and wait, listening, aware, peaceful.
9 Now come out of the meditation gently, but keeping the knowledge that you can direct light wherever you want, whenever you need to, to light up your life or someone else's or any dark or confusing situation.

Shine light on to your depression to see where it's coming from

The light is a reminder to waste no time being resigned to your depression. Instead get straight in there, shining light on it to see what's causing it. Sometimes, just acknowledging depression and fears and facing up to them can be all it takes to lighten your mind, and even when the causes are complex this recognition is still the first step to understanding and recovery.

Depression can be triggered by a trauma or hurt – redundancy, the shock of discovering you or a loved one have a serious illness, an accident, a burglary, or something long forgotten or hidden from your past – all kinds of things can be the cause. But all are about fear. You get through the crisis, but it strikes fear deep into your heart and mind. You tell yourself everything's OK now, but you don't believe it. You're always looking round the next corner, expecting another disaster to be lurking in wait.

Taking a long, objective look at this underlying fear is the starting point to dealing with it. As you do so courage, hope and perspective will come into the picture.

Live in the moment and take charge

The light will help you stop obsessing about worries. Keep it in mind to remind you, whenever worry surges, that the past is gone and in the reality of the present you simply need to live the best way you can. Pay attention to the message of genuinely protective fear. You can't stop old memories and imaginary fears flitting into your mind, but you *can* refuse to let them settle there. Say no to them and think about or occupy your mind with something else.

Think of your depression as a detective story – and solve it

Every depression is unique. When you are depressed, behind it will be a totally individual set of triggers, ongoing and accumulated reasons, symptoms and potential resolutions and healing strategies. So while it can be soothing and therapeutic to talk to friends and medics, however much they think they know about depression they, like you, can't possibly have full understanding of your particular situation until some comprehensive detective work has been done. A friend who blithely assumes a cause and says something like: 'Get rid of your boyfriend, he's causing your unhappiness', may or may not be right but even if his presence in your life isn't doing you any favours, he's not the sole reason you're depressed. You can safely bet that fear is behind every aspect of it and, if you keep this in mind and remember it's a protective emotion, you can start working out what really is wrong and what you can do about it.

So think of the light and how it symbolizes your ability to illuminate darkness and get to the bottom of it. Be your own detective – search out what's causing your depression, how to resolve the causes, how to heal and revolutionize your outlook.

Reasoning and research

It may well mean looking back into your past for causes or to see if something about your upbringing predisposed you to recurring depression. Memories that surface can be difficult to cope with and I recommend finding a counsellor you like, respect and trust to support and guide you. A good counsellor can herself be like a shining light to help you through this journey. Facing fears that have been haunting you and negatively affecting you in the present dissolve when realized and dealt with. Dealt with? This can be by forgiveness of others or yourself, understanding and compassion. Sometimes you won't be able to leave them behind for ever – but you will know that should they resurface you can instantly be aware of them and let them go again instead of being haunted and depressed as a consequence.

The kind of counselling known as 'cognitive therapy' is great for moving on. Seeing what's wrong with your life currently and working out improvements is hugely confidence-building, and action soothes fear. You are taking stock; you are looking at problems sensibly; you are paying attention to both detail and the whole picture. You are washing your fear right through and hanging it up to dry. Depression – what depression?

It isn't a dream . . . living in the light can be your reality

Chasing fear out of your life like this will soon become second nature along with a calm ability to enjoy all the light and love of the present. Soon, calmness and happiness will become the natural way for you and your depression will have disappeared.

From now on remember negativity shrinks and often disappears completely when we turn and face it in the light. Remember to say to it, 'Hey – thank you for warning me – but I don't need you now.'

Love yourself and be true to yourself

Whenever I work with someone who swears there's no obvious explanation for the fact that he doesn't feel right, who seems to be digging his heels into the depression, and who isn't willing to do something constructive to heal, it often turns out there's some kind of incongruity in the way he gets on with himself, his loved ones and his life.

We humans are adept at shoehorning ourselves into lifestyles and situations we know, somewhere deep down, we don't want to be in. We'll do a jolly good job of trying to convince ourselves it is right, or 'should be' right. But it isn't. So there's an unintentional but very

84

real dishonesty flowing through our world, which like the proverbial ill wind doesn't do anyone any good. So fear protests, big time.

'You've got to do something about this,' it pleads. 'At the very least acknowledge what's going on!'

But if you don't or won't heed fear's warnings, what's to happen? Perhaps you might lead a numb, masked life. Or you sink into depression first as a comfort because you're ill, you tell yourself, so you don't have to deal with the situation or look behind it to the truth. But then you get stuck there, or climb out but keep slipping back in.

Face the truth

The only way to free yourself from this type of depression is to shine light on the fear that's begging for attention by gnawing at you, and on whatever incongruity it's calling you to unravel. I can't tell you it's easy, as it takes huge courage to face the fear initially. But I can tell you this starts a flow of courage that comes automatically once you stop denying the truth. Just admitting what's going on makes you feel better immediately. Maybe you can't yet face changing your life, or maybe you decide it wouldn't be fair to others to do so anyway. That's OK – it's your decision, you are at the controls. But a decision made in truth will assuage fear.

Shine light to find and live in the truth. When you deceive yourself by believing in mirages or wearing a mask, fear will give you a hard time because it knows you aren't really coping – you're sinking. Listen to it – and surface.

Strategy

Begin to find out more about the real you: who you are; how you relate to others, and why. You can do this with help from books (see 'Further reading') or with the support of a counsellor. Self-understanding can come in flashes or swathes of insight. We're always growing so we're always learning. Go with the learning curve instead of resisting and, though by no means always easy, it feels good.

Fill your life with light and love – light up the path you're treading

Love and light are the opposite of fear. So fill your life with love for yourself, your friends, family, work and interests, and you'll go a long way to driving out fear. At the same time it feels good to love, so what with the dissolving of fear and the addition of love you'll also go a long way to sweeping depression out of your life, even when it has physical causes.

Help it all along with inspiration and creativity. What makes you feel good – or would, given the chance? To paint, or write, follow a craft or make music, to swim or walk, to cook? To be in flow with your creativity is to be in touch with the Creator you believe in or the energy behind this world. So we feel alive when we're doing something creative and it automatically lifts us out of depression and lights up our lives.

The healing power of light on mind, body and soul

The light is also a symbol reminding us we need lots of light – real light, that is – for our health and *joie de vivre*.

Avoiding seasonal affective disorder

Quite simply, if we don't get enough daylight we're likely to lose vitality. Light prompts the pineal gland to make serotonin – the hormone-like substance often known as 'the feel-good factor'.

> Get out in the light every day, or most days, (taking care not to burn). Half an hour or so will make a big difference. Natural light feels good, makes the world look lovely and supplies essential vitamins. If you are house- or office-bound in daylight hours, consider using a full spectrum light instead.

Light up your life with laughter and other good things

If I'm feeling listless or glum, and the light is the gift that comes to mind when I ask which one I need, I'll use it first to look and see if fear's behind the mood. Often, it's not – it could simply be a temporary hormone swing or low blood sugar. But when we're low, we pretty soon become fearful even if we weren't to begin with – so it's better to do something about the mood fast before those fears get out of hand and make us say or do something we wish we hadn't.

This is my check list to lift a physically caused mood or depression:

- If a hormone surge or dip is the culprit, seek out the appropriate alternative therapy – the right vitamins, homeopathic or naturopathic remedy can work wonders restoring the balance (see Chapter 8).
- Laugh about something – really laugh. Seeing the funny side lightens you up.
- Exercise – get your circulation going with a planned work out at the gym, a brisk walk or any aerobic activity you love. It has several benefits: blood flows round your body carrying oxygen to all the cells and you feel good because you're looking after yourself and also because mood-lifting hormones surge. It really does feel as though you've 'turned the light back on'.
- Clear some clutter – sorting out a whole room or just a drawer, simultaneously helps clarify any confusion hanging around in your mind. Much of your fear will be thrown out with the rubbish and you'll feel worlds better.
- Clean something. It could be you – a lovely long soak in the bath is always soothing and healing. Or the car or house, windows especially. There's something about cleaning that lets light into your soul. You just feel better for it.
- Give something away. Your time, your help, a loving gesture. Giving unblocks the channels of our lives and lets our natural healing ability flow through.

Do something to let the light stream back in. Use your light to remind you.

Thousands of depressed people hold onto the concept of 'a light at the end of the tunnel' and it really can be a bright star of faith to keep you going. And please don't be cynical. A depressed friend once said to me, 'Jenny, I think about the light at the end of the tunnel and get worried it's a train coming towards me.' But – it made her laugh and she immediately felt better!

Think of your symbol of light and let love and laughter shine through you and the world around you.

11

A crystal: changing the vibes in tense situations

The crystal is not necessarily the best or most influential gift but, for me, it's the one that can change everything in a heartbeat, that opens our hearts and souls to the potential and power of all the equally precious gifts we have. I'm especially fond of the crystal because it was my 'first gift', working swiftly and proving a great starting point in any uncomfortable situation. Of course, your special symbol may be different.

I remember feeling awed and joyous when I first saw my crystal. I knew something had happened which was profound and would touch my life with wonder and the means to make a positive change whenever I repeated it. Others too have been enchanted by the symbol of a crystal, feeling, as I did, that it enabled us to connect with this intrinsic gift we all had: the ability to change the mood in a place, within ourselves and/or between people, just by focus and thought. Just thinking of the crystal is enough to start the transformation.

When there's fear in the air, the crystal symbolizes your power to shift it

You know the feeling: you walk into a room and immediately sense tension. The fear could be yours or someone else's. It could be masquerading as anger, depression, jealousy or any of the other negative emotions. But however well hidden it is, you pick up on it. Fear may prickle through you physically, sending a shiver down your back or causing a headache, or make you miserable or uneasy.

When someone gets edgy with someone else, they respond by being equally or more sharp. However subtle or masked, immediately the element of fear in the air grows.

Transforming the situation

With the image of the crystal in mind it never fails to astonish me – and I know you'll be surprised too when you try it – how easy it is to improve relationships and ease tension by a simple shift in attitude.

Instead of thinking negative thoughts, when you remember the crystal you switch into positive mode. Immediately, you feel better, as though the emotional content of the atmosphere around you has changed. Instead of blaming, shaming and generally grousing about everyone else's bad behaviour and how uncomfortable the situation is, imagine shaking the crystal over the room and all the people there including yourself. See it shedding light and love, understanding and compassion and be aware this new energy – whether it comes from you or is harnessed from other dimensions that flow through us all the time – will home in wherever it is needed.

Instantaneously, the atmosphere lightens

How does this happen? It has a lot, perhaps everything, to do with body language. The moment we wish someone or a situation well instead of ill, our faces, posture and subsequent words and actions change. However subtly this happens, others notice the difference and normally spontaneously respond in kind, warming to you and becoming more tolerant and even understanding and sympathetic.

I believe that, as well as having an effect on our body language, every thought we think influences the atmosphere around us. Whether by body language alone or more, it's clear that when we think positively, with good intentions towards those around us, our interactions and relationships normally change for the better as a result.

It feels like magic but it's a very normal reaction

When you think of the crystal and see its effects, it feels magical. But in fact it's a very normal reaction which we can all set in motion because it's an ability we all have.

Try it! Next time you are aware of an uncomfortable atmosphere between you and others, think of the crystal. You may like to see its colour – one that to you seems appropriate for help, soothing and healing.

Imagine the light of the crystal transfusing the air around you and the people you're with. Think lovingly instead of defensively and/or aggressively. Think lovingly when you're decidedly not feeling loving? Yes – it is very possible. You have the ability to choose how to react to how you initially feel about any situation. And there is always potential for choosing another feeling, another attitude. Make it a positive one. You can summon the love and light within you even in the face of anger and darkness. I'm not asking you to be a saint – of course you can't just start loving someone who's currently a cause of hostility, but all you need to do is think of the crystal, choose an outlook of goodwill and send a wave of warmth to the other person and yourself.

Why use a crystal as a symbol?

It is both an ancient and a modern belief that crystals are endowed with transformational and healing properties. Many people say they can feel the energy coming from a crystal when they hold it in their hands. As a symbol they catalyse my personal power to effectively dispel or safely manage both fear and its causes.

There is also another practical physical effect: the multifaceted surface of a crystal bounces colour and light in all directions, and we know that colours and light have tremendous healing and energizing properties. In her book *Lifelight* my sister Dr Penny Stanway tells how the ancient Egyptians and Greeks constructed temples with domed ceilings of crystals that directed specific colours to rooms used for healing, childbirth or meditation. Today's scientists have proved what was known thousands of years ago – that light and colour affect the levels of various hormones and neurotransmitters in our bodies.

Are we really so powerful?

Absolutely. Sometimes stories illustrate how one person can transform a situation, and their own emotional state, however dire. Consider the movie of Charles Frazier's book *Cold Mountain*. It looks set to be a miserable-feel movie. Jude Law's character Inman is on a hard, long journey facing one catastrophe after another. Nicole Kidman's Ada is bereft, helpless and hopeless in her mountain ranch. Then in bounces Renée Zellweger's Ruby and the effect she has on the situation and her fellow chief protagonists in the movie, and on the audience, is extraordinarily uplifting and an excellent metaphor for the gift you have which the crystal symbolizes. Suddenly it becomes a feel-good movie, just because she sweeps in with a bright, let's-get-on-with-it-and-enjoy-it-as-best-we-can attitude. Even when she too faces disaster, bereavement and then potentially the loss of her friend to the returning Jude, she metaphorically shakes her crystal as she determinedly sets about changing her attitude back to a feel-good one. The minute she appears, you sense that however sad the movie is, there will be an uplifting resolution and there is.

Any one of the characters could have harnessed their own ability to transform their bleak situation. You can spring yours into action too and the crystal is there to remind you.

Cherish your crystal and use it often. You will change your world.

Good places to use the crystal

Whenever you sense tension or trouble in the air

You're a sensitive person – you wouldn't be reading this book otherwise. So you are sensitive to others' moods, and the emotional climate of places too. When you sense discord or bump into someone and they say with a bright smile, 'I'm fine', but you know they're really not fine at all, even when there's no concrete evidence, hold the image of your crystal and ask its help.

You will change the mood in the place. Without even saying anything, you will help the other person by sending her positive energy to lift her spirits and you'll go some way to healing whatever's wrong.

Whenever you're in need of a lift

Thinking of the crystal keeps us in contact with our power to lighten ourselves up and surround ourselves with an invisible protective shield.

Ask yourself how you're really feeling. Imagine that you have an aura of light around you (as some people believe we do).

Is it bright, vibrant and sustaining? Do you feel charged and alive? If so, then that truly is fine. Shake the crystal for good measure and get on with your day.

But what if your energy is sluggish or you're depressed? Then straightaway think of your crystal. Imagine polishing it up until it glows with life. Shake it around you, over your head, under your feet and out into the atmosphere until you're surrounded in millions of bubbles of light. See them sparkling with colours of different hues, fizzing with energy, banishing your blues.

You can do this. You do have the imagination. And by taking the leap of faith you will trigger your very real ability to energize yourself and, I believe, the air around you. You can recharge your self, your soul, your life ... the crystal simply symbolizes this ability.

Imagine you have your own crystal

1 It's already beginning to glow as you think of it.
2 Shake it and its energy will flow through you, all around you and beyond.
3 Let it motivate you to change your attitude to positive.
4 See how this automatically lightens the tensest atmosphere.
5 Think what else you can do to help change things for the better.
6 Send healing thoughts out to the others in the situation.
7 Think how you can turn this energy into practical strategies too.
8 Think how you can deal with fears until they dissolve if unneeded or, if they are a warning, transform them into constructive thought about how to deal with the causes.
9 Think of the crystal again to help summon the courage and hope that come when you face and work with your fears, realizing they are there to protect you.
10 Think lovingly. If you just can't, think how you can bring love into the equation, even simply by giving yourself, in your mind, a hug for encouragement. Remember that in the end everything good – everything – comes down to love.

Use the crystal. Don't forget. Whenever you sense even the slightest disturbance in your peace or that of other people, imagine it in your hand and then shake it so the energy flows and is broadcast all around. We catalyse the negativity in the atmosphere, grounding anger and all the other uncomfortable emotions – everything, in other words, that's based on fear – and bring in understanding and positivity.

If you are thinking that I'm just a very fortunate fruit loop who gets so much inspiration, joy and healing from my imaginary crystal, remember the crystal is a metaphor. But we all have the ability to pick up on others' moods and sense the atmosphere in places and between people. The crystal is a good reminder that you can help dissolve negativity and respond to its cause constructively.

Practise sensing the emotions around you

The more you use the crystal the more easily you will tune in to moods – your own and those of others. To get an understanding of how to do this, think of those times when you've felt positively joyful. Choose one and imagine yourself in that state now. I love this description by the composer Iasos, quoted in *Our Shared World* by Brad Steiger:

It sparkles in a manner that makes you feel very light and exhilarated. Imagine millions of tiny bubbles of light, all exploding with the happy desire to raise your vibratory rate. However unlike liquid this energy totally passes through you, filling the mostly empty spaces between all the electrons of your being.

He believed his creativity suffered when he was depressed and 'vibrating at a lower level' and said: 'That is why I try always to cruise on my usual higher vibration of happiness.'

We defuse fear and hate when we choose an attitude of optimism and love. Remembering your crystal can be a big help in taking this attitude and being ready to welcome in joy, inspiration and creativity.

Tune in to feelings of inspiration
and happiness and joy

You may feel excited for no particular reason – you know that lovely feeling when you sense the day ahead may hold something special for you, although you can't think what? Or when you have an idea that makes you sparkle inside? When this kind of pleasurable excitement fizzes, focus on it – really feel, enjoy and follow it. Not all ideas come to fruition and special happenings don't always follow its promise, but the buzz you get from going along with the feeling of excitement will give you energy and health and be great practice, too, for when ideas do progress. Meanwhile, enjoying the feeling will stretch and keep supple your capacity to be happy. Just as in physical health, our emotions need exercise to keep them strong and fit. We tend to think feelings are beyond our control but in fact we can use our minds not only to encourage but even create a mood of our choice, or we may decide to say no to feelings we don't want. It's all about being aware of our feelings and treating them positively, enjoying their variety and richness. We have tremendous emotional capacity and intelligence and, with a little effort, can find most of the time a comfortable, healthy emotional balance. Mind and heart work best when they're working in tandem, complementing each other and in harmony.

Stuck in fear when nothing's really wrong?

So often, a state of fear is something we get stuck in when the original cause has long since disappeared or been resolved. The crystal reminds us how we can restore a feeling of well-being and freedom from fear. Fear can be a habit – we get used to constantly looking over our shoulders, uneasily wondering what's going to happen next. But just as fear can be habitual, so can happiness – and wouldn't you rather be happy?

Happiness isn't so much something given to us when we get something new or have a particular personal success, which can make us feel great but it is a temporary high. Habitual happiness is an attitude we can choose to take, and we can make it a habit. Saying the glass is half full rather than half empty is the classic example and almost everything can be viewed from a glum perspective or a happy one. Seriously glum people can't even enjoy their good times – they wonder instead how short-lived their happiness will be and anticipate the next down. But choosing the half-full rather than half-empty mind-set is as easy as flicking a switch – you just have to remember to do it.

Even when you've turned the tables on fear and substituted the habit of happiness it's easy to slip back into chronic fearfulness. So we have to be on guard not to let negativity sidle back. You don't have to navel-gaze perpetually, simply be aware of it as soon as you get stuck into any anxious or glum mood. The crystal is a great reminder that you have the ability to choose your attitude – a positive one.

How can you tell if a bad mood is a habit, or based on real fears?

Sometimes just focusing on the mood and asking what's behind it is all it takes, if it's habitual fear, to see it's not real and blow it away.

Ask yourself if you feel as good as you could. If you do, that's great. But if you're aware of any unease, follow these steps:

1 Focus on the feeling.
2 Check out your body to see where it's centred.
3 Breathe into it.
4 Relax your muscles – especially your neck and shoulder muscles and any other of your favourite places for storing tension.
5 Ask yourself if there is anything you need to feel cautious or fearful about.
6 If there is, follow it through, making sure in your mind it's being taken care of – if necessary make a list of things to be done.
7 If you can't immediately think of anything, think of your map and your compass and check out your current situation. Are you where you mean to be? Are you happy with the direction you're taking? Are there any signs you need to pay attention to?
8 If the answer to the first and second question is no, or if you give a yes to the third, make a mental note to give the problems the attention they need.
9 If it's yes, yes and no, respectively, and all is well, breathe a deep, thankful sigh and shake off the unease like this.
10 Think of the crystal and its light and energy. Say firmly: 'All is well, and I have no need to be fearful just now.'
11 Thank the crystal and the life energy it symbolizes for your well-being.
12 Feel positivity sparkling through you.

Don't be afraid to shine – let the crystal remind you

You are a unique human being, beautiful in your own special way and talented in your individual style. We all have times when we fear we're hopeless, and probably a bit of humility and uncertainty is a good thing, now and then, but generally we need to boost our self-esteem by believing in and encouraging ourselves. Use the crystal to help – let the energy for good which it symbolizes flow around you and through you. Let your light shine, don't try to hide it. Not only will your own fear disappear, but you will help chase fear out of the lives of the people around you. Shine on . . .

12

A heart: fill your life with love
and wash fear away

So often, when you ask for the gift you most need in a moment of
fear, the symbol of a heart will come to mind. It signifies love, of
course, and it means to remind you of your ability to immeasurably
improve the dynamics of any situation or relationship by thinking
lovingly. It means you are to have compassion, to forgive, comfort
and soothe, and to help address and resolve fears. We all have this
ability – and yet it's so easy to forget all about it – even when we
need it most.

I know this and mean to be loving – and yet so often at some stage
of the day I forget. I guess most of us do for we're not naturally
loving all the time. Things happen and all kinds of emotions arise in
response. Frustration, anger, dislike, hate even. All, in some way, are
to do with fear. We're human!

Feel the fear, ask for the right gift to use –
the heart comes to mind

Just as fear is the opposite of love, so love is fear's antidote. We
can't go around in a permanent state of love – we're not saints. In
fact it's good we have a wide range of emotions – it means we're
aware, rounded people capable of empathizing with others.

But whenever fear and the negative emotions that tell of it make
us feel decidedly less than loving, we need to pay attention quickly,
and the heart is a fantastic gift in reminding us to let love back into
the equation.

If we think lovingly – or even, if this is beyond us in the emotion
of the moment, simply think of the symbol of a heart – it causes a
fundamental change in our outlook and attitude, balancing extremes
of negativity or hostility and letting love-encompassing traits such as
charity, fairness and insight weigh in too. Just like the crystal, the
heart seems to have a power of its own to affect situations and
interactions dramatically or subtly for the better.

Love is the opposite of fear

And love is more powerful than fear. So if you think of love, in some way, whenever you are frightened, the fear will retreat.

Love is an astonishing catalyst. Use it and we lose fear. But we forget! How does that happen – how can we forget? Or, sometimes, we lose faith in it or even deride it. 'Huh!' you hear cynics scoff, 'Love! I don't even know what love is.' Have you questioned or belittled love? I guess most of us have at some stage – either when we feel hurt, our self-esteem was low, or perhaps just under peer pressure to be cynical.

> Let's make a decision now never to belittle love again. Nor to confuse it either, as so many do, with 'in-love' passion, romance and lust. But to recognize it as the strongest emotion we can experience and a power that flows through us all the time.

Think of love and we tap into it. I believe an eternal supply is there for us, for ever – it will never run dry, never betray us. Love harmonizes, heals and unites us. It soothes difficulties, enables solutions, lifts us out of trouble or – when that's not possible – helps us tolerate it and stay strong and focused.

How to use the gift of a heart

Love is a joy and a gift we all have. We have the inborn ability to love and be loved and to connect with the power of love throughout our lives. The symbol of a golden heart is a crystallization of this.

1 Use it each and every day.
2 Every time you feel less than loving, imagine holding your gift, a small golden heart, in your hand. Feel the pleasing shape of it, and its solidity.
3 Ask for its help.
4 Think how you can be more loving – of yourself, of the others around you, of your world – whatever is needed right now.
5 Let love flow through you. Imagine it flowing through everything and everybody around you, energizing, healing, soothing, gently but powerfully replenishing courage, hope, trust and confidence.

6 Know it is making and will make a difference.
7 Take a moment just to think of love, and feel it.
8 Say thank you and let love make its impact. It will. Know it.

Use the heart as a symbol to remember how love can transform a situation or relationship

When you're about to say or do something meanly critical, picky or harsh, stop and be aware of the fear behind your impulse to do this. There is always fear behind unkindness. What is it telling you? What is it about?

Consider the effect you will have if you carry on being unpleasant to someone:

* How are they going to feel?
* How will they react?
* How would you like yourself or your sister/father/friend to be treated this way by someone else?

Now think of the symbol of a heart to remind you to act with love instead. If you were in their shoes, what you would like to happen that would make you feel good about the two of you? An alchemy happens when you put yourself in the other person's shoes. Immediately you see them and yourself in a completely different light. Obviously, you'd each like the other to be pleasant to you. Imagine feeling pleased, both of you, to be interacting positively.

What's stopping you from being pleasant and warm to them? It's how, deep inside, you actually want to be and if you set this very real, true part of you free, you stand to transform the situation into something positive and good. For almost certainly if you change your attitude and behaviour and become your reasonable, thoughtful, sensible, caring persona, the other person's behaviour will automatically mirror it or at least begin to adjust in that direction.

If the stand-off between you has been going on for some time, they'll naturally enough be surprised by or even feel suspicious about the change in you. Feel the fear and don't let it throw you; just keep being the real, nice you. Once they see they've nothing to lose and lots to gain from your new attitude, they'll thaw out fast and, in time, start to trust it's not a sham.

However, if the other person is habitually awkward and obstreperous and continues to be so, don't waste time and energy feeling scared and perhaps angry that the love is not working. Acknowledge that you feel scared – it's natural and understandable. Thank the fear for its warning and act on it constructively. You might ask the person to pretend to be you to gain some awareness, and to think how they would like you to be. They may laugh, scoff or outright refuse to your face. But the chances are, unless they have a clinical imbalance, they won't be able to resist doing what you ask out of sheer curiosity and humanity.

And then the alchemy will work, illuminating the situation for them just as it did for you.

Using your gift

Whenever you're scared, unsure or sceptical, hold that little heart in your hand and know that love will work its magic if you give it a chance. Think love. Ask love to help you out. It will.

The energy of love and light is powerful and transformational – pure gold.

How love catalyses fear into positivity and calm in animals and people

Use your gift of a golden heart whenever you sense unease, discord, sadness or some unknown fear within yourself, other people or animals. Think of its meaning – love and peace – and the situation will somehow change for the better as your body language and behaviour change and, I believe, the energy of love flows around you.

Picking up on others' emotions – and your own

'How are you?' you ask.

'I'm fine, thanks,' they answer.

But somehow you sense there's something not quite right about them. You have just an impression of unease, or anger, or sadness. Or perhaps you get a physical feeling that makes you uneasy – a sweet, sickly scent you don't recognize; a sense of a fabric brushed the wrong way, although you're not touching anything like that; or a prickle like electricity making the hair on the back of your neck tingle. As we have mentioned before, you're picking up on a physical manifestation of their unrecognized or hidden negative emotion.

People are often sensitive to this kind of energy and most don't know what it is. They brush the feeling off because they don't understand what it is or where it's coming from. But so doing contributes to fearfulness, because the troubling sensation puts the defence mechanism on alert.

These 'energy waves' have a number of names. The Ancient Greeks called them 'glamours', meaning 'deceptions', and in contemporary psychological jargon they are collectively known as 'affect contagion', describing how you 'catch' the feelings that others are transmitting.

Another way you can recognize others' hidden emotions is if you suddenly, for no apparent reason, feel emotional. If someone is hiding something or being dishonest or, unbeknown to you, behaving incongruously you may find yourself suddenly angry or suspicious, even though on the surface everything seems fine. Some people say they can also sense or 'see' others' auras, the magnetic energy field that surrounds them.

Animals sense these behaviours or emotional energy waves much more fluently than we do. Household pets, especially dogs and cats, have amazing antennae for them. Horses are perhaps the most sensitive of all. As highly evolved animals prepared to flee, they are fine-tuned to danger and perceive hidden feelings as alarmingly dangerous.

Fearfulness causes more negativity

The problem for animals and for those people who are highly sensitive to other human beings' feelings is that their fearfulness may cause them to react in a negative way. Horses can bolt, shy, buck or, like people, be downright aggressive all because they are scared. Then the discordant person reacts in turn and a negative emotional spiral is under way.

This is one reason it's vital to be aware of what may be going on. When you experience a sudden, confusing emotion, consider it. Where's it coming from? You? Or could it be the other person? Tune in – to your fear, and theirs. Some conversation, empathy or just a willingness to understand can clear the air and ground the glamours, at least for yourself.

Horses as healers

Helping others recognize and deal with their own fear isn't easy and may not be your mission. Perhaps then, if you get close enough to them, you could suggest they get the help of a counsellor. In the USA, several psychotherapists, counsellors and healers who are also experienced natural horsemen are bringing in horses to help, and are having outstanding results. Somehow people always choose a horse to work with who mirrors and/or connects with their personal kind of fear, helping them recognize their feelings and release fear safely. As well as being sensitive to emotional energies and problems, horses are also past masters at helping us recognize them – and then we're halfway on the road to understanding, resolution and healing.

After reading Linda Kohanov's ground-breaking book, *The Tao of Equus*, I travelled to California to participate in one of her workshops. The rapport and empathy between ourselves and the horses was phenomenal, helping us break the bonds of all kinds of fears. On the last day we danced with the horses, blossoming in a new phase of understanding and sensitivity to emotional resonance within ourselves, with others and with our fellow creatures. The love among us – people and horses – was palpable.

This learning and wisdom is growing in the UK too and, if you love horses or would like to know them better and want to expand your understanding of yourself and others and your ability to release fears, I can't recommend this kind of therapy and healing highly enough. It is as though the horses are teaching us about love and how to spread the message of love as an antidote and hugely effective translator of fear's messages.

New wave horsemen or, in popular jargon, horse whisperers, such as Linda Kohanov, Pat and Linda Parelli, Monty Roberts, Mark Rashid and Klaus Hempfling, are all first-class riders and trainers who have become people trainers and leaders too.

When you're approaching a horse, Parelli instructor Ingela Sainsbury says: 'Put your heart in your hand.'

When I remember to do this with my horse, Queenie, if she's scared or uppity, her eyes and attitude immediately soften towards me. 'Oh, it's you. Yes, you're OK. I can trust you,' she says as she relaxes.

With people too, when we remember to put our heart in our touch, words, actions, the atmosphere gentles, enabling harmony and love.

Use your golden heart

Just thinking of love taps you into its flow and instantly empowers you to soothe and encourage yourself and others and to defuse tension. Whatever is needed at this moment in your interaction with someone else or within your own self will come to you. Think of the symbol of the heart – think love – and love will make a difference. Do it – now and often – and see for yourself. I can't explain how it works, I only know it does.

Remember – think love and fear flees.

Dealing with personal safety fears

The heart is often the symbol that comes to mind when we're physically afraid. When you're stretching your limits in a potentially dangerous sport or activity, feeling a surge of love for yourself or tuning in to the support of a companion can be all it takes to give you courage to respond in the best way to the fear. The heart reminds you to take care of yourself, the right kind of care. It starts with risk assessment, which sounds lengthy but in fact need only take a few moments thought. What is the danger here? Is it wise to stop in your tracks, get help, or forge ahead? Remember, with the symbol of the heart in your mind, that courage comes as we take action.

Coping with global fears

We live in an age where tremendous hope for a better world rides alongside some deep fears. Threats such as terrorism and global warming are constantly with us. How can we, individually and together, deal with such immense fears?

When you are frightened, pay attention to the fear, ask for help and wait for a gift to come to mind. Many of the symbols are helpful in managing such apprehension constructively but I find the heart is usually the one that helps me deal positively with the fear in the moment and think of something constructive to do as well.

With love in your heart you can contribute to the search for world peace in many ways. Not least is to live peacefully in your own community. Remember the ripple effect – every kind word or action will have an ongoing effect that may one day travel around the world, helping in ways you can't begin to fathom.

In your local community too, you can encourage others to think lovingly, positively and constructively of ways to help make a difference. With prayer, and such actions as lobbying governments to pull together to distribute food, wealth and work, we can individually and together build a better way forward. World fears are like any fears; they need to be acknowledged and addressed in the best and most appropriate way.

You can make a difference. So feel the fear and deal with it constructively by doing something good to help others and the world.

It *is* possible!

Whenever you feel thoughts of bitterness at terrorists and others who threaten peace amid and among nations, recognize the fear and remember the symbol of the heart. Let it remind you of the greater power of love. And pray for peace on earth and goodwill between all people. As our prayers join together, they will become more vigorous, fired by and strengthening the inestimable power of love

---

Your attitude, perhaps almost imperceptibly, will change and join with a tide of goodwill, bringing people and nations together in the fight against terrorism, which is an extreme form of bullying.

Love is the only way and it will save us from ourselves.

Part Three
Your gifts, your choices

The 12 symbols remind us of gifts we all already have. It's fine to choose different symbols if you would like to and, if so, you can enjoy deciding on other items which are easily visualized and will best remind you of your innate abilities.

You may wish to follow the same guided visualization that first gave me the idea for using symbols to help deal with fears. It's a relaxing pleasure to follow the journey it describes. Suspend disbelief and imagine yourself really being on the path and visiting and talking with the wise one and you will find answers or new insight into whatever is presently on your mind.

So a few paragraphs below I set out my version of the journey to the wise one. Whether you or a companion read it aloud or you record it so that you don't need to, leave plenty of time in between stages of the journey and the visit itself. This will allow you to fully visualize and sense the path, and the meeting with the wise one, the answers and your gift.

Besides its symbolism, you may be interested in the symbolism of the story and what it means to you personally. Usually we already know the answers we seek and this is a way of bringing them to the forefront of our consciousness.

The 12 core symbols cover most of our potential fears and difficulties and when I make the trip to see the wise one, it's usually one of these gifts that is given to me again. It's funny how, familiar as these symbols become, they continue to surprise with their aptness or the way they highlight a particular slant of a situation. The gifts continue to give pleasure and often a surge of excitement along with welcome recognition whenever they appear.

But I expect that sometimes, like me, you'll find you are given a brand new gift. Its symbolism won't always be immediately apparent. Don't fret about what ability it signifies, or why you need to use it – you will understand it all at exactly the right time.

An unusual gift – what did it mean?

Last year, just before my course in California, I did the wise one visualization with friends and the gift I was given was a little gold terrapin. I remember saying, bemused, afterwards: 'A terrapin! What on earth is that all about?' I forgot all about it.

The trip to California was going like a beautiful dream, except that the accommodation I'd booked in advance was a huge disappointment. A tribe of cats and dogs were temporary residents, and their night's purpose seemed to be to keep me awake.

After a sleepless night, I knew I had to do something or fatigue would ruin everything. I lay in bed, able to see only two options, neither good. I could ask the animals' owners to find other accommodation for them or I could move. 'Why am I facing this horrible noise?' I thought in poor-me fashion and abject fear. And then I remembered to ask which gift would help me find a solution. Instantly, the terrapin came to mind and I realized what it meant: I could make my home anywhere, whatever the circumstances, because home isn't a place, it's the resting place of the soul.

So next night I relaxed, donned ear plugs, and told myself there was nothing to be frightened of, I could sleep soundly through the noise – it was only cats playing and dogs barking, nothing to worry about. I thought of my safe 'terrapin's shell' – a roof over my head and a warm bed – but most of all my ability to totally relax now I'd accepted the circumstances I'd decided not to change.

Later I was even more thankful for the gift of the terrapin symbol. Two charming women taking the same course arrived to stay and we immediately made friends, also ganging up for dinners out with the owner of the ranch house. We had great fun together and I learnt so much from each of them. Without the terrapin I would have moved to an impersonal hotel and missed it all.

Whatever gift you need to use and whether the fear is a spectre of your imagination or a protector sensibly cautioning you, when confronted, fear will dissolve.

A reminder of how to use the symbols

When you face the fact that you're frightened and ask for the right symbol to help, it will instantly come to mind. You will be reminded of your ability to deal with the difficulty or potential problem. It's an easy and effective way of freeing yourself from fear and remembering how to deal capably with whatever caused it.

1 Ask yourself which symbol you need.
2 Wait.

3 One of the 12 or a new one will come to mind, possibly followed by others.
4 Think what it means.
5 How can using it help?
6 Be prepared to wait for understanding – its usefulness will be revealed at just the right time.
7 Trust the power it signifies – your inbuilt ability to help yourself.

Your inner guidance will not fail you – it's an ability you have, yours to tap whenever you need to, a vein of gold in the body of your life.

The wise one meditation

Your gifts will come to mind as you need them, all you have to do is ask which one you need. But it's good to visit the wise man or woman now and then, especially when questions in your life are begging answers you presently can't find. And who knows – a new gift may come to you just as the terrapin came to me.

A note on preparation: make as sure as possible you won't be disturbed – unplug the landline phone and switch off any mobile phones. Then all you need to do is sit quietly, close your eyes and relax. To help you to do so, you may like to meditate for a few minutes or simply take a few deep, slow breaths.

Imagine that you are walking along a path through some woodland in the countryside. It is in the evening but as there is a full moon you can see the path clearly and your surroundings. What is the path like? How does it feel under your feet? Is it level, or sloping up or down? What can you see around you? Are you alone or do any people or animals join you as you walk and keep you company along the path? How do you feel as you walk? Take time to register your impressions and your feelings.

Now you come to a side track that leads over a bridge and then follows a slight upward slope. This is the path to the clearing where the wise one lives. Be aware of your surroundings as you walk towards the clearing.

When you arrive, leaving the wood behind as you walk into the clearing, you see a small camp fire in the middle, burning brightly, and the wise one is sitting beside it, tending it. Go up to him (or her), greet him, and then sit down by the fire and put a log on it yourself. As the fire lights up your faces, look at the wise one and take some time to be aware of his presence and your surroundings in the clearing – and of the warm welcome and compassion you sense in this place.

Now ask him a question about something that is on your mind and important to you. Then listen quietly to what he says to you in answer.

Now imagine that you are the wise one, listening to and advising this person who has made a long journey to come and see you. How do you feel about this visitor and their question?

Take time to feel and be aware.

And now be yourself again. Is there anything else you would like to clarify or ask?

Listen to the wise one's answer. Then continue to sit with him, in the warmth of his peace and understanding, for a while.

Now it's time to say goodbye to the wise one and you both rise. Before you say goodbye, he gives you something to take home with you, placing the gift in your hands as you hold them out. Look down at the gift. What is it? How does it look? How does it feel in your hands?

Tell the wise one how you feel about the gift and thank him.

Now leave him, and walk from the clearing back down the path. Be aware of your surroundings, and any companions on the journey back. You rejoin the main path and follow it until you leave the woods and reach home, still carefully carrying the gift.

Settle yourself down and take time to look at the gift again. Look at it closely. Touch it. How does it feel? What does it mean to you and for you?

Now imagine you are this gift. What are your qualities? What power or energy do you possess? How will you help this person? How can they use you and appreciate you?

Be yourself again. Imagine putting the gift away carefully in your memory. Know that you can call on it whenever you need it. Say goodbye to it for now and open your eyes.

Value the insights you receive. Value the gifts which tell of the abilities you already have and currently need to use.

Just as allegorical stories can tell us much about life and our world, so the symbolism of the wise one visualization and the gifts you are given will tell you much about yourself, your inner wisdom and ability, and your life's journey.

Above all, they are a pleasure to use. They switch the lights on. They make you remember what deep down you already know: you are effective and powerful, capable and sure.

> You have all the gifts you need to live your life to the full.

Further reading

These books have all helped and inspired me in some way while writing *Free Your Life from Fear* and in my life generally and I recommend them wholeheartedly:

Freedom from fear ...

... in our spirituality, creativity and inspiration

Cameron, Julia (1995) *The Artist's Way*, Pan

I couldn't put this book down until I'd read it from beginning to end. I pick it up again whenever I have doubts about my creative ability. It's a dance of fear-dissolving support and inspiration.

Csikszentmihalyi, Mihaly (1992) *Flow: the Psychology of Happiness*, Rider

You read this thinking 'Yes!' We know we need flow in our lives – most of us just need reminding. Mihaly Csikszentmihalyi does this with gentle, fascinating persistence as well as suggesting how to encourage it in.

Gibran, Kahlil (1996) *The Prophet*, Wordsworth Editions

If you haven't read this, do. If you have, read it again. Often.

Lamont, Gordon (2004) *The Creative Path*, Azure

Leading you to a vibrant way of living, working, playing and managing fear creatively.

'Two Listeners', ed. A. J. Russell (2000) *God Calling*, John Hunt Publishing

Whenever I'm frightened by large fears, trivialities or anything that disturbs my happiness and confidence in any way, I go to this book. Always, it tells me exactly what I need to know to deal with whatever's bugging me and to restore love and calm.

Walsch, Neale Donald (1999) *Conversations with God*, Book 3, Hodder & Stoughton

Another must-keep-reading book. It fascinated me, made me think, affirmed much I already knew vaguely and taught me a lot more. It takes a leap of faith to let go of scepticism as you read, but do it – it's worth it. Joyous.

... in self-esteem and freedom from personal fears

Gawain, Shakti (1998) *Living in the Light*, Bantam Doubleday Dell

This changed my life when I first read an earlier edition over a decade ago. It's just the loveliest book – another I like to reread.

Hay, Louise (2003) *You Can Heal Your Life*, Full Circle

A treasure for healing and growing your self-esteem. I reread it every year to remind myself of the wisdom.

Kohanov, Linda (2001) *The Tao of Equus*, New World Library

Kohanov, Linda (2003) *Riding Between the Worlds*, New World Library

You don't have to be a rider or know anything about horses for them to help you. In these ground-breaking, deeply compassionate books, Linda Kohanov tells how she found healing and transformation through the astonishing empathy and wisdom of horses, and how she now leads others in their own journeys of self-development and general understanding to freedom from fear.

Seymour, Jane (2003) *Remarkable Changes*, Regan

Jane Seymour's gentle strength, courage and *joie de vivre* inspire you to accept change and seek out new possibilities and opportunities.

... in our health and healing

Nicholas, Michael, Lolloy, Allan, Tonkin, Lois and Beeston, Lee (2003) *Manage Your Pain*, Souvenir Press

Don't tolerate another minute feeling hopeless and helpless about pain – read this book and take control of your fear.

Kenton, Leslie (1998) *Passage to Power*, Vermilion

If you're frightened of ageing, read this book. I did and the mid-life I'd been so wary of is a breeze – truly the prime of my life so far and I'm hoping the last third will be just as great in its own way too!

Stanway, Penny (2001) *LifeLight*, Kyle Cathie

Light, like love, is essential for our physical and emotional health. A beautiful book about the power and wonder of light.

... in the business world

Franks, Lynne (2000) *The Seed Handbook*, Thorsons

If you're anxious about starting a business, this common-sensical but still inspiring book takes you through the fear threshold into courageous decisions.

Roddick, Anita (2000) *Business as Usual*, Thorsons

Anita Roddick's writing is like her presence – amazingly motivational and a breath of fresh air. She is such an inspiration on so many fronts.

for practical ways to deal with fear

Cohen, Pete (2003) *Fear Busting*, Element

A plethora of practical techniques for coping with all kinds of fear.

Farber, Barry J. (2001) *Dive Right In*, Pan

A series of easy-to-read passages on turning pessimism to optimism, fear to challenge, apathy to excitement. I only have to dip into it to replace negative thoughts with 'Yes!'.

Fiennes, Ranulph (2003) *Beyond the Limits*, Little, Brown

Fiennes, Ranulph (1994) *Mind Over Matter*, Arrow

For anyone who ever feels less than strong. Whenever I'm physically scared I have only to think of what Ranulph Fiennes and his companions went through on their epic expeditions and I toss my head, summon my personal power and try to stop being wimpish. I don't always succeed but it makes me feel better!

Jeffers, Susan (1997) *Feel the Fear and Do It Anyway*, Rider

Courage flows when you read this book.

Maltz, Maxwell (2002) *The New Psycho-cybernetics*, Souvenir Press

How to free yourself from inhibitions that hold you back, and live more courageously. Clever, cognitive-oriented and a great read.

Herman, Judith, (1997) *Trauma and Recovery*, Basic Books

A landmark book for survivors of terror in understanding the effects of trauma and the process of healing.

... in our relationships

Bradshaw, John (1992) *Creating Love*, Piatkus

John Bradshaw's insight into our fears and difficulties with love inspires tremendous understanding, deep healing and greater ability to love and accept love.

Buscaglia, Lee (1984) *Love*, Souvenir Press

Leo Buscaglia was a most amazing man. He writes about love so enthusiastically and wisely you wonder how we can ever forget to live lovingly. When we remember, fear simply doesn't stand a chance.